# 1960s
# AUSTIN
# GANGSTERS

## ORGANIZED CRIME THAT
## ROCKED THE CAPITAL

JESSE SUBLETT

THE
History
PRESS

Published by The History Press
Charleston, SC 29403
www.historypress.net

Copyright © 2015 by Jesse Sublett
All rights reserved

First published 2015

Manufactured in the United States

ISBN 978.1.62619.840.1

Library of Congress Control Number: 2014958076

*This book is dedicated to Lois Richwine*

# Contents

# ACKNOWLEDGEMENTS

I want to thank all the people who helped me with this book, particularly, as always, my wife, Lois Richwine, and my son, Dashiell Sublett. I also want to thank my mother, Elizabeth Sublett.

Special thanks are due my great friend Eddie Wilson, whose vast knowledge, wit and wisdom have been assimilated into every page. I'll also acknowledge my appreciation for the guys I call The Knuckleheads, which should not detract from my assertion that I value their infinite wisdom and counsel in matters of writing, chicken-fried steak, sweet potato pie and boxing (not necessarily in that order), their names being David Marion Wilkinson, Kip Stratton, Tom Zigal, Jan Reid and Christopher Cook.

This book would also have been impossible without the great help and resources from the Austin History Center, the Briscoe Center for American History at the University of Texas and the National Archives and Records Administration in Fort Worth.

Thanks also to Christen Thompson, senior acquisitions editor; Katie Stitely, editor; and everyone else at The History Press. The author photo is by Todd Wolfson.

Unfortunately, a tight deadline and space limitations prevent me from giving proper acknowledgements to every person who lent support, large and small, to this project. An incomplete listing of names will have to suffice for now, but please know that I do appreciate your support: Debi Dabbs, Laylee Muslovski, Betty King, Marc Abel, Nick Kralj, Douglas Swanson, Joe Nick Patoski, Johnny Reno, Peggy Imbert, Bill Gammon, Roy Q. Minton,

Charles Schotz, Richard Zelade, Jesse Freeman, James Tolbert Jr., James Cooper, Terry Gardner, Walter Dollar, Johnny Hughes, Manuel Estrada, Velia Estrada, Mike Cotten, Mike Graham, Ramiro Martinez, Harvey Gann, Ronnie Smith, Kay Beasley, Carol O'Quin, David Fox, Gregory Curtis, Kim Simpson, Barbara Rust, Dick DeGuerin, George O. Jackson and many others.

Finally, a second big thank you to Debi Dabbs, Laylee Muslovski, Betty King (and the girls) and the daughters of Sue Overton, because I know it wasn't easy.

# INTRODUCTION

Tim Overton reached the peak of his football career with the University of Texas (UT) at the Cotton Bowl Classic on New Year's Day 1960. A sophomore on the reserve list, he got no field time in the game against the Syracuse Orange. It was just as well. Before the crowd of 75,500 fans, the all-white Texas Longhorns went down 23–14, defeated by a small, integrated New England college that fielded several outstanding African American athletes, including Heisman Trophy winner Ernie Davis. Texas also exacerbated its humiliation by inciting an ugly racial brawl in the second quarter.[1]

Never mind that now. Having played football for UT still carried enormous prestige, and it remained part of Tim Overton's identity for the rest of his short life—even after he achieved notoriety as the leader of an infamous Austin gang of safecrackers, pimps, drug dealers and Cadillac-obsessed hoodlums.

The Overton gang was Austin's locally grown white trash mafia, with heavy connections to the Italian counterparts in the Big D, Cowtown, the Little Man in New Orleans, Biloxi, Oklahoma, Florida and Chicago. At least two other ex-football stars were part of that team.

It was the '60s, and Austin was beginning its evolution from sleepy state capital and college town to the creative class/music mecca we know today. Austin natives are so proud and protective of our city's reputation for coolness that we adopted the slogan "Keep Austin Weird." Did the coexistence of counterculture and thug culture help make Austin cool?

*Above*: The Austin Motel on South Congress Avenue today. For several decades, it was a magnet for prostitution and vice. *Author's collection.*

*Left*: The State Capitol Building in Austin; with its pink granite dome, it is taller than its counterpart in Washington, D.C. *Author's collection.*

"It was a good place to party," said musician Gerry Storm. "Austin had a reputation for being a beautiful, rather colonial place," different from the rest of Texas and a destination for "rich kids…as they waited for their inheritances." And even before there was any kind of a music scene, much less something to brag about, Austin was different because it was "snobbish, a city of tea sippers," home to "an underground of irreverent scholars, artists, and politicos—some of them with national reputations—that you don't find in any city."[2]

"It's an important part of Austin history," said Nick Kralj, former club owner and longtime Austin backstage historian. "You always had a connection with the outlaws and the lawyers and the politicians," said Kralj. "It was all connected because they all like the same things. You know, whores and booze and other stuff like that."[3]

My introduction to the Overton gang came from the microfilm archives of the *Austin American-Statesman*. The year was 2002, and I was researching a series of murders in 1976 by a serial killer in which my girlfriend, Dianne Roberts, was one of the victims. That story was incorporated into a book titled *Never the Same Again*, published in 2004. A crime story headlined "Police Feel Deaths Gang Action" told of two Austin hoodlums, John Soriano and Henry Travis Schnautz Jr., murdered gangland style within hours of each other. Schnautz was a former associate of Tim Overton. An eight-hundred-word background article, "Austin Underworld of the '60s: Overton Gang Capers Recalled," made me feel that I had stumbled onto the secret history of Austin.[4]

*Ghosts of the notorious Timmy Overton gang, an Austin-based underworld outfit involved in drugs, prostitution, bank burglaries, jewel thefts and other crimes in several states in the 1960s, may be haunting police again in the gang-style slayings of Travis Schnautz and John Soriano.*

*James Timothy Overton, an Austin native and star football player who eventually was accused of numerous crimes, was the titular chief of a large group of pimps, prostitutes, drug dealers and burglars which began organizing in the 1960s. The gang—including the infamous Jerry Ray James, one of the FBI's 10 most wanted men until his arrest in 1968—was believed to have staged more than 30 bank burglaries and numerous other crimes in several states before law enforcement officers cracked down on 20 of its principal members in a massive federal conspiracy indictment in 1967.*

Soriano turned out to be a minor figure, but Travis Schnautz was an old-school hood. Since the mid-'50s, he had bounced between burglary, haircutting, pimping, the music scene and drug dealing. His record showed more than fifty arrests and several prison terms. He was busted in 1957 for selling five pounds of weed to a narc for the Elvis and Edsels–era price of $350.[5] Travis and his wife, Robyn, were good friends of country singer Willie Nelson—a reminder that the music scene has always been a magnet for fringe characters and illegal activity."[6]

I soon learned that Overton and his best pal, Jerry Ray "Fat Jerry" James, were co-captains on dozens of bank burglaries in small towns, mostly in West Texas, Kansas and Oklahoma. Overton's father owned a transmission shop in East Austin, which served as a headquarters for the gang and doubled as a safecracking lab.

People who knew Overton described him as smart, funny, generous and charismatic. Fat Jerry, also a former football star, got mixed reviews. "Jerry Ray James was a vicious, brutal sociopath who didn't have any redeeming qualities whatsoever," said attorney Roy Q. Minton.[7]

Others apparently found James to be tolerable, even hilarious, especially when he was with Overton. "The two of them together were like a vaudeville act," said Betty King.[8]

Probably the closest the gang ever came to becoming nationally famous was during the federal conspiracy trial referred to in the *Statesman* article. Overton and James were among the fourteen men and six women accused of running a multi-state bank burglary and prostitution ring. The case went to trial in Del Rio in early 1968 and concluded there the following June.

*The indictment alleged that 14 men in the gang burglarized 18 banks in 1964–66. It also charged various gang members with six bank burglaries in Kansas and one in Oklahoma and other crimes in Colorado and Mississippi.*

*Six well-known Austin prostitutes were also accused of conspiracy. The women allegedly accompanied the men to areas where burglaries were planned. If any of the men were arrested, the women allegedly raised funds by prostituting themselves in order to post bonds for their men.*

At a time when the war in Vietnam and civil rights made questioning authority feel like a moral imperative, the Overton gang confronted authority as a lifestyle. When Tim Overton discovered a hidden microphone in his wall heater vent—shades of the post-9/11 surveillance state—he filed a federal civil rights suit against the Austin

One of the small-town banks victimized by the Overton/James gang in the 1960s. *Courtesy of the NARA, author's collection.*

Police Department. A second scandal erupted when it was revealed that a sophisticated recording system had been installed in the county jail.

Unfortunately, on the date that the *Statesman* reported Overton's illegal surveillance lawsuit, the big feature was an incident at a South Congress Avenue bordello owned by Austin's leading madam, Hattie Valdes. "Gangsterism—Austin Style: One Night at Hattie's" told how Tim Overton and his shotgun squad had moved to take over prostitution in Austin but were beaten back by the police and rival pimps. Tim Overton the thug had upstaged Tim Overton the civil rights champion.

Even if the Overtons didn't affect the direction of culture in Austin, they were certainly part of it. With their caravans of Cadillacs, pinkie rings, expensive suits and alligator shoes, they made an impression wherever they went. They smoked pot long before it became a political statement, and they patronized the coolest clubs in town, along with some of the most disreputable. Bandleader Henry "Blues Boy" Hubbard told me that Overton tipped him $100 at a time, but go-go dancers got twice as much.[9]

**TIM OVERTON**, guard, should be a tough man for the opposition to handle next year.

Let's be clear: these guys were not admirable citizens. Tim Overton and his friends were violent, predatory and brutal. Their tracks are sometimes easy to follow because they left a trail of abused victims and destroyed property. The last thing I'd want to do is to romanticize them, but they were interesting people living during an interesting time. Many, if not all, of the men came from dysfunctional backgrounds and the kind of circumstances that tend to foster feelings of powerlessness and low self-esteem. In a perverted way, learning to control others through intimidation and violence might have felt like personal advancement.

*Top*: Tim Overton, who attended Austin High from 1956 to 1957, had a bright athletic career ahead of him. *Courtesy of the* Comet, *1957.*

*Left*: Tim Overton in jail, 1966. In every photo I've seen, he has the same strange, unfocused expression, as if he's mentally somewhere else. *Courtesy of the NARA.*

# A NOTE ON TERMS

Overton's network of criminal cohorts and camp followers included two brothers, his father and stepmother, hence the use of the name "Overton gang" and sometimes "the Overtons," particularly in the Austin area. In places where Jerry Ray James was better known, members of the media took to calling them "a modern-day James gang."

By the mid-'60s, law enforcement agencies from New Mexico to the Florida coast had begun to recognize the existence of a sort of alternate mafia, particularly in the South and Southwest, where the Italian mafia had gradually lost ground. Rather than being a centralized crime syndicate, Tim Overton, Jerry Ray James and their colleagues were part of that network. Police bulletins began referring to them as "traveling criminals." By the end of the decade, the term "Dixie Mafia" was being applied to the same people.[10]

The Dixie Mafia has been the subject of several books and movies over the years, but the subject matter is almost exclusively about later periods, as opposed to the era in this book, the '60s. For a short discussion of books and films about the Dixie Mafia, please see Appendix 2.

# 1
# GETTING EVEN: 1956-1961

In the '50s, before the Austin skyline was a clutter of high rises, the Capitol and the University of Texas Tower were its undisputed defining landmarks. You could see them and know that you were in the capital city, the home of the University of Texas.

Every summer, young boys went down to watch the Longhorns in their preseason workouts, drilling, sprinting downfield in one-hundred-degree heat and jogging up and down the steps of Memorial Stadium. Mike Cotten was there, watching and dreaming. "I grew up wanting to be a Longhorn from when I was six years old," said Cotten. "I was watching them back in the 1940s. There was never any doubt about who I wanted to play for."

Tim Overton was there, too. Cotten and Overton were the same age but from very different backgrounds. Overton grew up in the East First Street neighborhood, home to a mixed population of Hispanics and working-class whites. Some of the streets were still unpaved. The Cotten family lived in a spacious, rambling mid-century ranch-style home on Belmont Parkway in Tarrytown, the west side of Austin, the prosperous side. The addresses were barely five miles apart, but they were worlds apart.

The Tower stood tall from the campus hilltop, a beacon marking a possible way out for Tim Overton. He wasn't a running back, a golden boy like Mike Cotten. Overton played guard on offense and linebacker on defense, positions where aggressiveness and a mean streak were key. He also fought in Golden Gloves. Boxing was another possible way out.

The University of Texas Main Building, universally known as "the Tower," stands higher than the Capitol dome. *Author's collection.*

For the poor and/or nonwhite, Austin could be a mean town in the '50s. Congress Avenue was the dividing line, with the haves on the west side and the have-nots on the east. Working-class and country people were often ridiculed as cedar choppers, stump haulers and white trash. Across the river from downtown, South Austin was still countrified, with north–south thoroughfares lined with feed stores, tourist courts, junkyards and beer joints.

Hyde Park, now solidly middle class or better, was a gritty neighborhood. As Eddie Wilson tells it, today's solid middle-class addresses once bred street fighters and hoodlums. "There were guys who went off to the pen for five or ten years," said Wilson, "and once they got out, they couldn't afford to live there anymore."

The Sixth Ward, east of downtown between Sixth and Eleventh Streets, was the official African American neighborhood. South of Sixth Street down to the river was the Seventh, home to a mix of Hispanics and working-class whites. The Seventh was also called East First Street (renamed Cesar Chavez Street in 1993).[11] Many Hispanics in the East First area had been forced to vacate other parts of the city that the city planners of the 1920s had designated for "whites only," the same policy that established the Sixth Ward as the official black section.[12]

In the '50s, the west side—with its clean streets, Greek Revival mansions and sprawling mid-century ranch-burgers—became the destination for teenagers from the poor side of town. They went cruising for dates, starting brawls and crashing parties. Every October 31, Tarrytown became ground zero for mayhem and madness. Water balloons, rotten eggs and other missiles were launched at cars and pedestrians. Street fights broke out.

Halloween 1956 would be remembered as a real "Hell Night." Burning tires were rolled into the street. A bunch of teens commandeered the roof of the Gulf station. Max "Fat Max" Roesch lassoed a cop off his three-wheeler. Don Jester cold-cocked a guy who turned out to be a plainclothes cop. Surviving participants include Dick DeGuerin, the renowned defense attorney whose high-profile cases in recent years have starred Willie Nelson, Tom DeLay and Clara Harris, a Houston dentist who killed her philandering husband by running over him in her Mercedes multiple times.

Dick DeGuerin was another flat-topped wannabe-thug following in the shadow of brawling, swaggering Austin High bruisers like Tim Overton, Don Jester, Jesse Freeman and Sonny Stanley. But on November 1, 1956, DeGuerin was taken aside by his father. "He told me I was headed for prison," DeGuerin told me, "just like those other guys."

Message received. DeGuerin entered an afterschool work program, graduated from Austin High in '58, enrolled at UT in the fall, joined a fraternity and avoided getting into trouble—unlike many of his former classmates. After graduating UT School of Law in 1965 and passing the bar, DeGuerin learned his trade at the side of the esteemed Percy Foreman, a titan of Texas criminal defense attorneys, and then became a legend in his own right, regularly defending clients who have committed vile, abhorrent acts.

*Above*: Calvary Baptist Church, circa 1937. Of the two little girls, left of center, Ima Nell has the blond hair, and cousin Mildred is at right. *Courtesy of Mildred Green.*

*Left*: Finus and Ima Nell Overton, Tim's parents. The photo was taken not long before her terminal illness. *Courtesy of Mildred Green.*

*Left to right:* Jack, Finus, little Tim and Ima Nell Overton. Jack was Finus's brother. *Courtesy of Mildred Green.*

Each year at the summer law class he teaches at UT, DeGuerin, a veteran of Hell Night '56, tells his students to always remember one important idea: "Defending people who do terrible things is an honorable profession."[13]

LIKE MANY OF THE WHITES who lived around East First, relatives on both sides of Overton's family were Depression-era refugees from West Texas. Financial collapse and the Dust Bowl made farming untenable, or, as Tim Overton's aunt, Mildred Green *née* Hinton, said, "the Depression was when the farmers just about starved to death." Even after moving to Austin, many of the Overtons, Huckabys and Hintons spent portions of the year as itinerant cotton pickers.

Tim Overton's parents, Finus Ewil "Snooks" Overton and Ima Nell Huckaby, met in 1937.[14] Freshly discharged from the army, Overton, age twenty-three, was still wearing his uniform when he saw young Huckaby playing hopscotch with his cousin Mildred Hinton. Huckaby was thirteen. "Snooks was immediately smitten with Ima Nell," said Hinton. Marriage followed a few months later. A first son, Charles, was born in 1939, followed by James Timothy the following year and three others: John, Darrell and Finus Jr.

The Overtons weren't the poorest family in the neighborhood, but there was always something unsettled in the household. "You'd see kids running around with just their underpants on," said Ed Wendler, who knew Snooks Overton as well as Tim Overton. "There'd be chickens in the yard, no screen door on the house." Wendler recalled Snooks Overton as "a rough guy...poor and ashamed of it" and abusive to his wife and kids.[15]

The Overtons moved often, sometimes in the dead of night. The city directory for Austin between 1940 and 1953 lists at least nine places. One year has "Overton, Finus Ewil" living in the back of a beer joint on East First Street called Pack Tote. Other addresses were 32 Canadian Street (present-day Robert T. Martinez Street), 810 Clermont Street, 2100 Holly Street, 1800 Haskell Street, 1504 East Sixth Street, 4716 East Fifth Street, 1811 Riverview and 1910 East First Street.[16]

Overton's classmate Pete Johnson was a neighbor when the Overtons lived at Chalmers Court, a New Deal housing project between East First and Fourth Streets.[17] "In the summer," Johnson said, "we would go up on the roof and sleep there under the stars."[18]

People who knew the Overtons said that Ima Nell Overton was the rock, the one who held the family together. An attractive, broad-shouldered woman with dark red hair, she attended every Little League game, track meet, Golden Gloves fight and football game.[19]

She also managed the transmission shop, or at least, she did until the spring of 1957. In July, she entered the hospital and underwent surgery for a type of brain tumor called astrocytoma, which is caused by mutations of star-shaped cells called astrocytes.[20] After surgery, she returned home wearing a scarf over her bald head.[21]

During what was surely a grim summer for the Overton family, the Austin High Maroons ratcheted up football practice in preparation for the season.

*Opposite, top*: Chalmers Court, where the Overtons lived for a time. Tuffy Korn and Pete Johnson also lived there. *Author's collection.*

*Opposite, bottom*: In the foreground on the left are Finus and Ima Nell Overton, with Finus Jr. on Finus's lap. *Courtesy of Mildred Green.*

*Left to right*: Darrell, John, Ima Nell, Charles and Tim, probably in Corpus Christi, 1951. *Courtesy of Mildred Green.*

Overton was starting is senior year. The Maroons had not won the state championship since 1951, but this year, hopes were high. The varsity squad was deep in talent, experience and size. Head coach James Tolbert, along with sports writers across the state, expressed confidence that this was the year the team would bring home the state trophy.[22]

Ima Nell Overton was hospitalized at Brackenridge again in late August. Kay Beasley (née Patten), then Tim's steady girlfriend, went with him to the hospital on Saturday, September 7.[23]

"I remember I had just given her a pill, a pain pill or something," said Beasley. "A few minutes later she coughed it back up. We called the nurse and they made us leave the room. I don't know if you've ever heard a death rattle, but that's what we heard, and you never forget it."

Sunday was Overton's seventeenth birthday. The funeral was on Monday afternoon, the first day of school. The six pallbearers were all Overton's teammates: Don Jester, Mike Cotten, Walter Dollar, Pete Johnson, Manuel Estrada and Heinie Pate.[24] Pate had to be excused from school early so he could buy a suit for the funeral, which he remembered costing thirty-five dollars. For a poor family in the '50s, that was a lot of money.

"Something snapped in Tim when his mother died," said Mildred Green, an observation I heard from numerous others, but Overton didn't drop out of school, nor did he end up in reform school or jail. Four days after the funeral, the Maroons played the first game of the season. During the pre-game pep talk, Coach Tolbert said they were dedicating the season to Overton's mother.

"I'll never forget it," said Walter Dollar, "Before every game Coach Tolbert would remind us that we'd dedicated the season to Tim's mom. He'd say, if you make a promise like that, you've got to go ahead and follow through. You don't want to dishonor her."[25]

Dollar was then a dark-haired boy from Hyde Park who played center. He made a point of being at Overton's side, just for good luck, whenever they exited the tunnel between the locker room and the football field.

From the first weeks of the fall of 1957, the Maroons seemed to have everything clicking—plays, teamwork, talent and luck. Playing like champions, they obliterated all their non-district opponents and ran over all their district foes. The championship almost seemed preordained, but in the quarter-finals against Port Arthur, on a rainy day on a mud bucket of a field in that East Texas oil town, the Austin Maroons collapsed before the Port Arthur Yellowjackets. So dismal was their performance, the final score of Port Arthur 14, Austin 6, could have easily been 50–6.

The *Statesman* began its post-game coverage by citing Winston Churchill, who once advised that crying wasn't necessarily a sign of weakness: "Probably none of the Austin Maroon football players ever heard Churchill speak, but they walked into their dressing room Saturday afternoon with their hearts very heavy. A dream had been shattered."[26]

"I haven't talked about things like this in a long time," said Maroons lineman Manuel Estrada, "but that trip home after we lost that game was heartbreaking. It's something we wanted so bad. One game and we would've been in the Cotton Bowl playing for the championship. It was just so damn heartbreaking."[27]

Estrada had known Overton since childhood, growing up in East First. He was one of several of the boys on the flight back to Austin who had trained and competed alongside one another in sports going all the way back to Little League. These same boys had long held Overton and his best friend, Don Jester, in special esteem because they were fighters, meaning they boxed and they also fought bare-knuckle, street-fight style. Six decades later, voices filled with grim wonder, men of a certain age still talk about those fights—the sanctioned bouts at Golden Gloves as well as the primal contests after school at Dirty Martin's, the Pig Stand, House Park or the rock quarry.[28]

"Whenever we watched them fight," said Walter Dollar, "there'd be a point when we'd say to each other, 'What if this turns out to be something we don't want to see?'"

In a notable convergence of rock 'n' roll and fisticuffs, Golden Gloves tournaments were held at the City Coliseum, the same multipurpose events center where Don Jester punched out a young rockabilly singer at the backstage door after his show in January 1956. The singer's name: Elvis Presley.

Ronnie Smith, Stephen F. Austin High School class of '58, told me the story. Why would Jester do such a thing, I asked. "Don was a rockabilly singer, too," Ronnie said. "He was jealous, I guess."[29]

And so, on that long flight back to Austin, one sight seared into the memory of their teammates was that of the toughest among them crying like babies.

"That was one of the few times I ever saw Tim or Don actually break down," said Manuel Estrada. "The majority of us had cried already, but Tim and Don, they were the last ones to cry."

The year 1958 would mark the second season for the Longhorns' new coach, transplanted Oklahoman Darrel K. Royal. Not yet a legend (as a coach, anyway), Royal was the new guy, the one who was under pressure to turn things around after 1956, the worst season in recent history: one win, nine losses.[30] Royal met with Overton in April 1958 to discuss signing a letter of intent to enroll at UT with a full-ride football scholarship.[31] The meeting was held at the Patten residence, where Kay Beasley lived with her mother. Overton and Beasley were no longer going steady, but they were still close friends. The Pattens lived at 2202 Sunnyslope, a quiet block of homes in Tarrytown.

"Mike Cotten and Darrell Royal came over to my house when they were interviewing him about giving him a scholarship," said Beasley. "I guess because they weren't comfortable with them coming over to his house. [Tim] came from a family that was, well, struggling."

Kay Beasley had never actually seen where her boyfriend lived. By 1958, possibly earlier, Overton was actually living with his maternal grandmother. In fact, after Ima Nell died, all the siblings except for the youngest, Finus E. Overton Jr., moved out. Beasley never knew.

After graduating, she attended UT, earned a degree, married and left Austin, worked overseas and, more than fifty years later, returned to Austin. We met for coffee. As she sorted through a box of high school memorabilia, she was startled to find Overton's graduation diploma and other keepsakes.

"I'll be darned," she said. "I wonder why he left these with me? Maybe he knew they would be in safekeeping."

Darrell Royal's mother had died of cancer shortly after he was born, and that fact had always haunted him. He must have felt empathy for Tim

Overton, but with a limited number of scholarships available, Overton's record of discipline problems presented a risk. By the fall of 1958, when Overton started football practice, his brother Charles was serving time for bank burglary.[32]

Overton got his scholarship to UT, as did Mike Cotten and Bobby Nunis. Five of their teammates accepted football scholarships to other colleges: Ronny Schulz, Rice University; Walter Dollar, Sam Houston College; Heinie Pate, UT Arlington; and Don Jester, Texas Tech.[33]

In March or April, barely six months since Ima Nell's death, Snooks Overton married a woman named Florine Craine. Her previous husband, Melvin Birch, had up until recently been the head mechanic at

*Top*: Tim Overton and Kay Beasley (née Patten) at a high school Christmas function in 1956. *Courtesy of Kay Beasley.*

*Right*: Tim Overton (number 62) and Walter Dollar (number 52) always took the field together for good luck, 1956 season. *Courtesy of the* Comet, *1957.*

Tim Overton, 1956 season at Austin High. *Courtesy of the* Comet, *1957.*

the Transmission Exchange. Craine had divorced Birch twice previously, making a total of three marriages and three divorces, and six children, several of whom remained in her custody. Over the next seven years, Craine divorced Snooks twice and married him a total of three times, the last one ending in his death in 1966 at the age of fifty-two.[34]

"Florine was already on drugs before she and Snooks got married," said Mildred Green. "After Ima Nell died, we went to Austin and stayed with Snooks for a while. Florine was hanging around the transmission shop then. My husband Jack could tell they were doing drugs and messing around."[35]

In the fall of '58, Tim Overton enrolled at UT with a major in engineering. His roommate at Moore-Hill Hall, the athletic dorm, was G.W. Martin of Waco. Both had been named All-District guards their senior year.[36] During a brief phone interview in 2004, Martin told me that for the first two semesters, his roommate took school seriously. "He made good grades, especially in math," said Martin. "He was smart."[37]

In the football program at UT, students were not allowed to play on the varsity team until their second year. In the fall of 1958, the freshman team, the Texas Shorthorns, enjoyed an unbeaten season. Overton and quarterback Mike Cotten made the cut.[38]

"He had gotten real, real big," said Charles Schotz, one of Overton's high school friends from the west side of town. "He always had a big jar of

Darrell K. Royal on the left with the coaching staff, 1959 season. *Courtesy of the* Cactus, *1960.*

Bennies and a fat money roll in his pocket. We had lots of fun. It seemed to me that he wasn't doing a lot of studying."[39]

The Longhorns finished the 1959 season with a 9–2 record and ranked number four in the nation. On New Year's Day 1960, Texas met the Syracuse Orange in the Cotton Bowl Classic in Dallas. The inclusion of African American athletes on the visiting team caused problems from the moment they entered Dallas, where hotels and banquet facilities were restricted to whites only. During the contest between teams, Syracuse won on points, 23–14, and class. Ernie Davis, one of several outstanding African American players for Syracuse, was honored with the Heisman Trophy. Texas, which remained an all-white team until the next decade, taunted the Orange with racial epithets and other unenlightened, unsportsmanlike conduct. During the second quarter, fights broke out as a result. The official line at UT was one of denial and attempts to blame the visiting team for being too sensitive.

The members of both teams received gold commemorative Cotton Bowl Classic wristwatches engraved with cotton bolls on the face, the final score on the outside rim and the players' names on the back.[40]

A DIFFERENT SORT OF PRINTING triggered Tim Overton's first serious felony conviction. A forgery scheme began with the theft of a check-writing machine at Al Ehrlich Supply Company, a lumberyard at 3201 South Lamar Boulevard. In the 1950s, forgery was a major crime problem on par with hacking and identity theft today. Check-printing machines offered a measure

The historic Broken Spoke, 2014, surrounded by development, the address of Tim Overton's first felony crime conviction. *Author's collection.*

of protection, but for a forger with a team of fast-acting check-passers, they were like analog ATMs.

A series of the company's checks had been cashed at Austin businesses. Two recent federal parolees, Charles Ray Overton and John Weatherford, were busted in the act and promptly snitched on Overton. As parole violators, they were returned to the penitentiary without trial.[41]

In September, Overton appeared before Judge Mace Thurman and pleaded guilty. Thurman, who was generally known as a strict law and order judge, gave the clean-cut, well-dressed, polite, contrite young football player two years' suspension. As customary, the provisions of his probation included a strict ban against associating with known criminals—such as a drug addict older brother who was going to rat him out.

In the fall of 1964, four years after the check-writing machine was stolen from Al Ehrlich Supply Company, James White built a low-ceilinged, no-frills, sawdust-on-the-floor Texas dance hall on the property at 3201 South Lamar Boulevard. James White, a Texas two-step aficionado recently discharged from the army, was originally attracted to the site because of the majestic old oak tree out front. Before the army, White's favorite venue for dancing and catching touring performers had been Dessau Hall, a popular dance hall located north of Austin where an oak tree stood in the center of the dance floor. White named the new place the Broken Spoke, inspired in part by a dream that his hero Bob Wills might play there someday. Not only did Bob Wills play there, but the Broken Spoke also became an Austin music landmark. Willie Nelson liked the Spoke so much he started playing there free.[42]

On October 15, less than three weeks after the first forgery conviction, Tim Overton was charged with aggravated assault. On November 22, a check-writing machine was stolen in a burglary at W.D. Anderson Company, a building supply outfit on Spicewood Springs Road. Once again, two known criminals were arrested for passing forged checks, and they ratted on Overton. On December 15, a Travis County court found Overton in violation of the terms of his previous conviction, and just before Christmas Day 1960, he was riding the bus to the state penitentiary in Huntsville.[43]

"Tim just always wanted to be a thug," said G.W. Martin. "He liked it. Part of it was that East Austin culture over there, that thug culture."[44]

Martin also mentioned Harben Leonard "Sonny" Stanley from the class of '58, plus other friends from the neighborhood who, instead of going to college, had gone to Huntsville. These ex-cons and other longtime thugs from East First were "bad influences," Martin said, but the worst was Overton's brother, Charles Ray.

Martin's assessment was echoed by others.

"When Tim's mother died, it broke his heart," said Pete Johnson. "That was the end of it for Tim. Then his brother Charles Ray came along. It's a shame Tim had to have a brother like that."[45]

George O. Jackson, now a celebrated art photographer, was a rebellious young college student who met the Overtons through his attorney friends and became a regular drinking buddy. He also had a pilot's license and co-owned a Cessna 210, and on their occasional flights to Mexico and elsewhere, they spent quality time together.[46] For Jackson, there was no mystery about why Overton abandoned the straight life: he felt abandoned and betrayed by Darrell Royal and UT.

"Tim idolized Darrel Royal, and Royal turned his back on him," said Jackson. "So he had it in for the whole system. I know this from observation because I heard Tim spout off about this many times."

Overton did more than just talk about getting even. Revenge figured into more than one of his criminal schemes. But before consummating his most famous act of revenge, he met another UT student saddled with bitter memories and

Charles Joseph Whitman enrolled at UT within two weeks of Tim Overton's release from Huntsville. *Public domain photo.*

grudges that eventually coalesced into a sick fixation on the UT Tower. His name was Charles Joseph Whitman.

Paroled in August 1961 after serving eight months, Overton returned to Austin and became involved in all aspects of the Austin underworld: drug smuggling, prostitution, burglary, strong-arm and gambling. It was about two weeks later that Overton and Whitman first met. Whitman would act on his own revenge fantasy five years later, August 1, 1966, committing the first public mass murder of the '60s. Seventeen were killed, thirty-one wounded. An excellent account of that tragedy is *The Sniper in the Tower: The Charles Whitman Murders*, by Gary M. Lavergne.[47]

Lavergne's book relates several incidents about Whitman's obsession with gambling. It turns out that Whitman was terrible at poker. He also tended to rack up gambling debts and then arrogantly refused to pay. Lavergne describes tense encounters between Whitman and "two ex-con brothers known in Austin circles as a very tough pair."[48]

When Lavergne wrote *Sniper in the Tower*, he had no clue about the identities of these "toughs." When I reread the book in 2003, it became obvious to me that the "tough pair" was Tim Overton and one of his brothers, probably Charles.

Too bad Lavergne never met Nick Kralj. In 1961, Kralj was a young poker hustler from Galveston and a freshman student at UT.[49] "I played poker a lot in high school, and I kept on playing in college," Kralj said. "Right away we had a game going at this dorm I lived in, Cactus Terrace. It was a private dorm. You weren't supposed to be playing poker in the dorm. It got to be a pretty good-sized game, and we got busted. We couldn't play there anymore. The guy who was running the dorm said, 'No more, I'll get you kicked out of school.'"

Subsequently, the game was moved to Goodall-Wooten, a high-rise dormitory across the street from the main mall of campus, in the 2100 block of Guadalupe Street, locally known as the Drag. Charlie was one of the freshman residents, and besides being happy to host the poker game, he was the hall monitor.

"We're playing up there with Charlie because he was in charge of Goodall-Wooten," said Kralj. "We thought we had the best deal going. We had perfect security because he was the guy who was supposed to enforce the rule about no gambling. Plus, he had money, but the guy couldn't play a lick. He was always losing."

The tone of the game shifted when the professionals got wind of it. "Tim Overton starts bringing in his guys," said Kralj. "Pretty soon they start

Tim Overton and a puppy, 1951. *Courtesy of Mildred Green.*

making some moves, as in cold decking and stuff like that. I didn't know for sure what they were doing, but they kept winning and Charlie kept losing."

Charlie Whitman ended up owing Overton about $200. He paid part of the debt by check, but the next day he called the bank and stopped payment. Tim and Charles came to Whitman's dorm to collect in cash. They threatened him with a knife.

At that point, instead of being cowed by the Overton brothers and their feared reputation, Whitman's behavior got really weird. He bought a .357 magnum and carried it wherever he went. According to Lavergne's sources, Whitman also looked into swearing out a peace bond against the Overton brothers.[50]

Whitman was an odd duck. In November 1961, he got caught butchering a poached deer in the shower at the dorm. Friends in the dorm heard him discuss his pet idea: going up on the UT tower with a deer rifle and shooting people.[51]

"One night, Tim wasn't in the game, but he came to the door," said Kralj. "Tim has the hot checks with him and he starts threatening Whitman. Whitman pulls out a pistol. I remember it was a .357 magnum. And I said, 'Oh shit. I'm going to get kicked out of school, maybe shot, be taken down to the police, it's going to be all bad news.' So Whitman tells Tim, 'Get the fuck out of here, I'll blow you away, don't come back.' He took the checks and tore them up. So Tim leaves and I know he's going to come back. I was going, 'God, if I can just get out of this room without getting shot or kicked out of school I'll never come back here again.' And so when Tim left, I said, 'I'm out of here.'"

Kralj gave up on playing poker at Goodall-Wooten. He never saw Whitman again either. "I often thought, how wonderful, I guess wonderful isn't the word, but if Tim had killed him," said Kralj. "I thought he was gonna kill him, but I guess he got distracted."

Overton was more than a little distracted: in March 1962, he and his brother Charles were picked up in the swanky Highland Park neighborhood of Dallas, which had been hit by a string of late-night burglaries. He was returned to Huntsville to serve out the remainder of his sentence.[52]

Tim was released again in July 1962. Returning to the rackets in Austin, he apparently had no time or interest in collecting a $200 debt from a geek at UT. Whitman also had to leave Austin for a while, being recalled to active duty in '63 and then obtaining a discharge in '65 in order to return to Austin and reenroll at UT.

On Monday, August 1, 1966, the day of the Tower massacre, Tim Overton was in Austin between bank burglaries and court dates. He had his own designs for getting even.

# "THE CREAM OF AUSTIN'S UNDERWORLD": 1962-1963

*Tim was a likeable fellow, but he was always trying to con you.*
*He had no conscience. He was a sociopath.*
*—George Phifer*

T im was a tragic story," said George Phifer. "He was ruggedly handsome, tall and wide and strong looking. He looked like he could run right over you." Phifer, who was the acting chief of police when he retired in 1992, sounded almost regretful when he told me that he was the officer who arrested Tim Overton for printing checks on the device stolen from Al Ehrlich's Building Supply Company in 1960, effectively ending his football career.

"Tim was a likeable fellow," he said, "but he was always trying to con you. He had no conscience. He was a sociopath."

On an unseasonably hot, moonless night, January 30, 1963, ten television sets went out through the back window of Steve's TV Shop, 4225 Guadalupe Street, right across the street from the State Hospital grounds. The investigation, headed by Detective William Flow, zeroed in on one suspect immediately, but over a month went by before there was any news about the case. Finally, on March 3, 1963, Austinites learned that "James Timothy (Tim) Overton, former Austin High School grid star, who went on to the 1960 Cotton Bowl Classic with the University of Texas Longhorns," had been charged and released after posting $3,000 bond and "declined to make a statement explaining how his Cotton Bowl Classic watch turned up at the scene of the break-in."[53]

The thieves entered from the back of Steve's TV Shop at 4225 Guadalupe Street. *Author's collection.*

As an ex-con, a guy like Tim Overton had to expect being accosted or questioned in public, or pulled over at any time a cop recognized him or his automobile. Typically, guys in the rackets had been playing tag with the heat since they were juveniles, and harassment was just part of the game. Between January 30 and March 3, Tim Overton had at least two such encounters with city police. On February 6 and again on the eleventh, he was charged with vagrancy, or NVMOS (no visible means of support). Vagrancy statutes in the South originated as Black Codes enacted during Reconstruction as a means of circumscribing the citizenship rights of African Americans. Austin's vagrancy statute gave police leeway in making warrantless arrests of known (or suspected) outlaws. It criminalized the outlaw lifestlye.

Joye Nalls, a former pimp and featherweight boxer, told me he got fed up with being arrested after driving home from the whorehouse or dice game, having to spend the night in jail and then have all his illicit earnings consumed by fines and attorney's fees.[54]

"I got tired of staying in jail," he said, "because my wife, I mean, my old lady, would be working out at Hattie's and I'd go pick her up, and I'd have seven or eight or nine hundred dollars when the sons-of-bitches would pick me up. And it would cost me two hundred dollars bond appearance, three hundred bucks for lawyer."

A dancer with a lust for life, Joye also eschewed drugs because, like the police, they got between him and the things he wanted to do. "They'd haul you in on what they called 'the suspicious persons ordinance,' too. They got me on thirty-two arrests, about twenty, twenty-five suspicions, with no charges. I got tired of it. I finally smartened up."

By the late '60s, Nalls said, he was "pretty much out of the rackets," by which he meant he was down to shooting dice, cockfighting and running a beauty shop.

One of the usual things about Tim Overton was his Austin rootedness. He bought new cars more often than he changed addresses and logged thousands of miles a month on gambling and burglary runs, but by comparison, even his roommates were nomads. You could tell by their arrest records.

Jerry Ray "Fat Jerry" James and Clifford Henry "Hank" Bowen worked the gambling, robbery and burglary circuit between New Mexico, West Texas and Oklahoma. During the Steve's TV Shop investigation, they were arrested numerous times in different cities.

Bowen—born in Lawton, Oklahoma, in 1931—was one of Overton's new fraternity of Huntsville acquaintances from the oil-rich, thief-abundant Permian Basin of West Texas. He was a footballer in high school at sixteen but dropped out before finishing tenth grade. Working in the oil fields, he became an expert at operating heavy machinery, an experience that sparked a preference for burglary and gambling. By the age of twenty-six, he'd done a prison term and two years in the army. He had a reputation in the world of poker and carried his "car salesman" business card with a wink and a smile.

Jerry Ray James, an ex-footballer born in Corpus Christi in 1939, probably deserves his own book. "Fat Jerry" was the most enduring of a long list of colorful nicknames and aliases of the five-foot, ten-inch, 220-pound thugster. His parents, Bernice and T.S. James, raised four other siblings, out of whom three did not go to prison (A younger brother, Jerome, later served as a logistics connection and fence in the Dallas area for many venture-capital fundraising trips). T.S. put in forty years with Aramco and then retired to Odessa, where at around the age of twelve, something snapped in Jerry Ray's head. In junior high school, "he received excellent grades…[but] was rather aggressive with his peers, lost his temper very easily, [and] was inclined to abuse others physically, resulting in a lack of acceptance among his associates."[55]

The Jameses shipped Fat Jerry off to St. Joseph's Academy in Abilene, a West Texas outpost of conservatism, Christianity and beef production. In the spring of 1957, Fat Jerry left the academy with a diploma and football scholarship to San Angelo State in hand. He attended college there from 1957 to 1959, but according to his record, college was mostly an opportunity to recruit teams of students in their teens or early twenties who possessed a similarly nihilistic bent. Smuggling large quantities of booze onto the college campus (hundreds of bottles at a time) was one thing, but other crimes bristled with the capricious rage of a West Texas dust storm. In one four-month period, burglary targets included jewelry stores, drugstores, gas stations and a roller rink.[56] Convicted of burglary on March 31, 1959, James received two years' probation. Within four months, he had notched six new arrests and other violations.[57]

At a hearing in district court in August 1959, the judge revoked Fat Jerry's probation, stating that to do otherwise "would render probation meaningless." After ten months in Huntsville, the bull-necked Odessan made parole and enrolled in Odessa College, where he redefined the word "meaningless" with his dogged pursuit of bootlegging, forgery, brawling, burglary, gambling, armed robbery, home invasion and prostitution. He did not finish the academic year.

"Jerry would go to the Cadillac dealers and test drive a Cadillac and drive it around as long as he wanted," said a woman who ran in the same circles in the '60s.[58] "The dealers wouldn't do anything because they were scared shitless of him."

Encountering Fat Jerry for the first time, lawmen were sometimes fooled by his phony identification card and "glib and smooth talking manner."[59] Under personal traits, FBI reports mentioned that he was egotistical; had a preference for silk underwear, "the better hotels" and expensive cars, particularly the big-engine V-8 Cadillacs, Chevrolet Caprices and Pontiac Bonnevilles; and for a time, had lived with an African American girlfriend.

From the Midland side of the Midland-Odessa "Petroplex" came Fred Clinton Hedges, whose career as a UT football player overlapped with Tim Overton's, prior to their overlapping terms at Huntsville. Back in Midland, they called Freddie "the Powder Keg 158-pounder." A Midland High School graduate, class of '57, Freddie carried the ball for the Midland Bulldogs whenever they were in a tight spot, needing a halfback who could run straight up the middle with the determination of a go-for-broke Permian Basin wildcatter, grinding a hole in the offensive wall like a tricone rock bit through hard shale.[60]

Hank Bowen, Tim Overton and Fred Clinton Hedges in jail again together in 1966.
*Courtesy of the NARA.*

Born in 1939, Freddie Hedges had deeply dimpled cheeks; a lopsided, "aw shucks" grin; and asymmetrical eyes. Freddie favored high-quality, sporty shirts and slacks and cashmere cardigans. Upon graduation in 1957, Darrell Royal recruited him for the Texas Longhorns. At UT, Freddie was also enrolled in the Army Reserved Officers Training Core, but after four semesters of low scores in academics, Royal sent the Powder Keg back to Midland, where his physical prowess found expression in the Midland-Odessa Golden Gloves competition. He fought as a welterweight in 1959 and 1960.[61]

Another fall-winter cycle in the Permian Basin, another youth crime wave. In February 1961, eight suspects were charged with stealing an estimated $20,000 in cash and valuables from Midland-Odessa-area businesses and homes in a four-month period.[62] Those arrested were Freddie Hedges, Fat Jerry James and an eighteen-year-old girl named Vickie Carruth, plus two other young men and three teenage girls.

According to the *Odessa American*, both James and Hedges "orally admitted a $1,000 safe burglary at Odessa College," which had occurred on January 31, 1961, when Fat Jerry was a student there. James and Hedges also admitted to their role in the majority of the fifteen other burglaries attributed to the group.

For the next year, the term "dormitory" would mean a wing of Huntsville for Fat Jerry James and Freddie Hedges. Freddie was released on parole in 1962, having served one year out of five. In 1964, he enrolled at Kingsville A&I. He earned solid B's one semester and all A's the next. In 1965, he transferred to Odessa College and made the dean's list.

The road to a college degree again hit roadblocks in the spring of 1966. Freddie confessed to his role in a March 1966 bank burglary in the Texas

Panhandle, resulting in, among other things, a position in the federal conspiracy indictment with nineteen other Overton/James associates who went to trial in 1968 (see chapters 6–8).

Back in the '50s, the only B that Freddie Hedges earned at UT was in a course titled "Bible: The Life of Jesus." Flashing forward a couple of decades, Freddie Hedges found religion and went into the oil business. There's a fearful symmetry in that chronology. The Permian Basin, with too much oil and too many churches, also gave us Jerry Ray James; Hank Bowen; Dandy Dan Hall; his little brother, Dale (of whom we'll hear later); and the George W. Bush presidency. [63]

During the Steve's TV Shop investigation, Dudley Edgar Pounds also got the standard treatment for known associates of Tim Overton. Pounds was a big bruiser from McCallum High, class of '58. When they were fifteen, Pounds and Overton played for the 7-Up Tigers in Austin's Colt baseball league. Jimmy Cooper, one year their junior, remembered Pounds playing catcher. "Dudley was big enough to stop not only a fastball but also a charging bull," said Cooper.

In January 1963, Pounds was arrested in a raid on a Baytown tourist court, where deputies seized more than $3,000 in cash, "500 pairs of loaded dice, gadgets for rigging roulette wheels," numerous guns and several varieties of narcotics.[64] A few weeks later, Pounds was arrested in Odessa with "four pairs of crooked dice and four decks of marked cards." Released after two days in jail, he was promptly arrested for speeding. His passenger was another Overton associate, Curtis Glenn Garrett. Pounds and Garrett got into a fistfight with the cop, resulting in another trip to jail.[65]

Curt Garrett, born in 1929, was a tall, big-boned, flat-topped ex-con from Tim Overton's book of reliable partners from the West Texas oil patch. Garrett cut a striking figure in his open collar and dark suit at the racetrack. He was almost TV star handsome. Garrett and Overton were arrested in Purcell, Oklahoma, in 1964, with handguns and other weapons in the car and a trunk loaded with burglary tools. When they were in custody at Purcell and, later, transferred to Odessa to be interrogated for a jewel burglary case, Garrett refused to make any statement except that the walkie-talkies in the tool bag were for deer hunting.

"Oh, I was impressed," said Betty King, remembering her first encounter with Overton and his friends. "They were funny and exciting. They drove big cars and threw a lot of money around."[66] A recent high school graduate from South Texas, King planned to attend nursing school, but money was short, so she decided to take a gap year or two and moved to Corpus Christi,

A safe that was opened with an oxyacetylene cutting torch. Photo included as evidence in the 1968 conspiracy trial, location unknown. *Courtesy of the NARA.*

the city on the Texas Gulf Coast named after the Son of God—ironically so, as in pre-European settlement times the area was inhabited by the Karankawa Indians, who were known to eat people.[67]

She found a job as a waitress in a bar. There was also a private-bar-within-a-bar that offered mixed drinks and games of chance. So King became a mixologist and began meeting interesting people. Overton, James and a bunch of other characters frequented the place when they were in Corpus. King found the whole bunch to be highly entertaining, but Curt Garrett, who was more subdued, more businesslike, was more her type. They hit it off. At first it was a romantic fling, and then business got involved. "I was his first prostitute," said King, "and he was my first pimp. So it worked out OK for both of us."

Garrett, a married man, gifted her with furs, jewels and good times at the dog races in Reno and Mexico. Betty did call-girl work and stints at the Chicken Ranch in La Grange before gradually transitioning to full-time nursing in the 1970s.

Safecrackers liked the term "busting" as much as "safecracking," which accurately described many of the methods employed to open a safe. Before going to all that trouble, however, the safecracker would carefully search the premises to see if the combination could be discovered (One of the most common hiding places was on the underside of a desk drawer). As for the physical methods of penetrating a safe, the outside walls of a laminated safe could be "peeled" open with the help of a grinder, after which it was attacked with punches or chisels driven by a short-handled sledge. The combination lock could be defeated by a method called "punching," which entailed the use of a power drill and the aforementioned punch and sledge.

The Overtons had an edge on some burglars in that they had access to tools from a legitimate business. Sometimes they would steal the whole safe, using the winch on the back of the Transmission Exchange truck. Later, the wrecked safe was dumped in a cow pasture and, frequently, rural cemeteries.[68]

Prior to the TV shop case, Tim Overton was the prime suspect in a burglary at Dan's Sporting Goods in Austin. The score included one hundred watches, seventy "Goddess of Love" diamond rings, thirty-four other diamond rings, $28,000 worth of loose diamonds, three cameras, scuba gear, guns and ammunition, adding to a total loss of more than $50,000.[69]

The police were impressed by the burglars' professionalism and "split-second accuracy." "They knew exactly what they were after and were in and out of there in no more than five minutes," said Detective George West. A description of the getaway vehicle, provided by a neighbor, sounded suspiciously similar to that of the Transmission Exchange tow truck.

The Cotton Bowl Classic watch being left at the scene of a burglary has stuck to the legend of Tim Overton despite being at least half false. What seemed to be a slam-dunk case fell apart when Tim Overton presented a solid alibi. All charges against him were dropped.

On April 9, 1968, during questioning prior to her testimony in the conspiracy trial, Tim and Darrell Overton's stepmother, Florine Craine (she had remarried after the death of Snooks Overton in 1966), provided the missing information (which I have verified through other sources): Tim had given the watch to Darrell. Darrell was wearing it when he broke into the TV shop.

> [Florine Craine] *stated when DARRELL WAYNE OVERTON broke in Steve's Television Shop at Austin, in which burglary he got ten new televisions in 1963 or 1964, he broke a wristwatch band* [and

*the watch] had TIMOTHY OVERTON's name on it. She stated TIMOTHY got this watch when he played in the Cotton Bowl at Dallas with the Texas University football team. She stated that the police "hooked" TIMOTHY OVERTON on it.[70]*

Florine Craine's pre-testimony interviews spilled a great deal of inside information about the Austin underworld, including matters such as the TV shop case, which fell outside the time frame of the conspiracy indictment (March 13, 1964, to April 30, 1966) and could not be mentioned during her testimony. Craine's pre-testimony interviews also provide telling details about the gang's prostitution business, including her own involvement.

*She stated that SUE JEAN, TIMOTHY's wife, went to some place in Oklahoma and hustled and sent TIMOTHY money to pay bond and lawyer's fees. She advised that in the other places where SUE JEAN hustled, SUE JEAN would send the money to her, Mrs. CRAINE, who would in turn give it to TIMOTHY. She stated this money would come to her at $200, $300 or $400 at a time.[71]*

Craine stated that she had known Sue Overton since 1962, which suggests that she and Overton may have been together since then. A petite beauty with long, blond hair and delicate features, Sue Jean Schumann was born in the rural town of Blanco, Texas, about a half hour's drive west from Austin. The father abandoned the family early. When Sue was eight years old, her mother left a note and stuck her head in a gas oven, leaving the child in the care of an aunt who had little time or inclination to nurture her. Sue Jean Schumann was "shipped off to Kansas to be married when she was fourteen."[72]

By 1962, her legal name was Sue Jean Smith. She was back in Austin with two young daughters and a son and a husband in prison. The daughters were born when she was married to a man named Eugene Wayne Morgan, who was killed during an armed robbery. When she met Tim Overton, she was lonely and needed help, said her daughters, who remembered their mother's new boyfriend as "tall…very charismatic…and scary."

Overton's approach was a traditional one. He seduced Sue Smith as a girlfriend, slowly tightening the knot of commitment, and then he turned her out. They were married on October 9, 1963, in Seguin, Texas.

During the 1968 conspiracy trial, in which Overton's wife was a defendant, Florine Craine stated that Sue Overton earned between $600 and $800 a week as a prostitute and delivered all the proceeds to Tim Overton. The

*Statesman*'s daily coverage of the trial reported that "all of Mrs. Overton's earnings were turned over to her husband, who was unemployed and attending college," but that is false; Craine was actually testifying about the time period between 1964 and 1966. [73]

It was almost standard procedure for a character to be in a relationship with a prostitute, but for the Overton gang, it was one aspect of an ongoing enterprise. Prostitution funds went for burglary tools, hotels, travel and running-around money but especially for legal fees. Whenever the heat was on or the men were in jail, their women had to work overtime to cover additional expenses.

The gang's prostitution business was also a boon for the federal prosecutor. When the girls worked out of state and transmitted their weekly earnings back to Austin via Western Union, they were committing a federal crime—using interstate commerce to transport illegal earnings and acting in furtherance of a criminal enterprise. Almost everything the women did in their line of work could be considered within the framework of a criminal conspiracy.

Two Austin detectives, Harvey Gann and R.E. "Ernie" Scholl, knew more about the Overtons than anyone else in Austin who had never done a prison term. Harvey Elwood Gann retired in 1983 after thirty-seven years with the Austin Police Department (APD), most of that time, as head of vice, narcotics and special services. Robert Ernst "Ernie" Scholl, who died in 2014, was a thirty-year veteran with the Narcotics Unit of the State Department of Public Safety (DPS). Gann and Scholl were the detectives who headed the joint task force investigation of the gang between 1964 and 1968, which culminated in the federal conspiracy trial of 1968. Starting in 2003, Scholl and Gann sat for many hours of interviews for this book.

Harvey Gann and Ernie Scholl had much in common, but in some respects, they were the odd couple. Scholl, the narc, did much of his work as a plainclothes, undercover cop under various guises, while Gann was the public face of the establishment, particularly during the culture wars of the 1960s. He was an old school square, bald-headed and smirking. He could have walked right off the set of *Dragnet* or a high school health film.

Fans of Austin musician hero Roky Erickson still detest the name Harvey Gann for his role in the first big drug bust of Roky's seminal psychedelic band, the 13th Floor Elevators, in January 1966. Here, Gann was one of the unapologetic figures behind the campaign to destroy not only the Elevators but also other advocates of the drug culture, underground political agitators and other threats to the status quo. [74]

Harvey Elwood Gann served for decades as Austin's top vice cop. *Courtesy of the Austin History Center, used by permission.*

Less well known, however, is the fact that Ernie Scholl was the cop who busted legendary blues musician Jimmie Reed in 1960, a year before his big hit "Bright Lights, Big City."[75] Reed was on his way to Galveston when his car was pulled over by the state narcs. Reed, his wife and three others were arrested for possession of a pistol, 192 barbiturate capsules and "other drugs," which were not identified at the time of the arrest. Reed had previously played shows in San Antonio, Dallas and Houston. Scholl, who was assigned to Houston at the time, received a tip that Reed's car was "loaded with stuff." Surprisingly, Reed was allowed to play his gig at the Pleasure Pier in Galveston, after which he was escorted back to jail. The next morning, he appeared in court and left for Detroit.

Harvey Gann and Ernie Scholl were both combat veterans of World War II, fighting on opposite sides of the world. Gann grew up in Del Valle, a community on the southeast outskirts of Austin. During the war, he served in the Army Air Corps on the crew of a B-24 bomber. On his fourteenth mission, his B-24 was shot down over Italy. The only member of the ten-person crew to survive, he was taken to a prison camp in Germany, but his captors found him to be a slippery subject. He made three escape attempts, which succeeded in varying degrees, and a fourth time in which he made it safely to Allied lines and was shipped stateside on May 7, 1945, one day before the official end of hostilities in Europe.

Ernie Scholl served in the navy in the Pacific as a backseat gunner in a torpedo bomber and, later, as a parachute rigger.[76] He started with DPS as a trooper in 1948 and worked his way up to the rank of detective. In 1953, he was one the five original agents assigned to the newly organized DPS narcotics unit. That's right, five agents for the entire state of Texas.

Scholl had been with DPS for fifteen years before he met Harvey Gann, and Tim Overton was the subject of the first conversation. It was early '63, and Scholl was still on liaison with the Houston Police Department. Lieutenant Harvey Gann called from Austin with a tip that Overton had just left Austin to make a buy from a known drug dealer on the outskirts of Houston.

Scholl set things in motion with unmarked cars tailing Overton and a stakeout on a tourist court near Katy, a railroad stop on Highway 290. Overton and his companion, twenty-eight-year-old Bobby Joe Ward—ex-con, safecracker and pimp—showed up for the buy. Seven pounds of weed in a burlap sack passed from the dealer's hands through the buyers' car window.

The logistics sucked. Overton and Ward sped away. Sirens wailing, three cop cars engaged pursuit down one-lane roads in a patchwork of flooded rice paddies. Overton and Ward finally pulled over. The pot was long gone. Found after an all-night search, it had soaked all night in muddy water, useless as evidence. The district attorney wouldn't touch the case.

During the arrest and booking, Scholl hung back in the shadows, maintaining his cover. Overton and Ward never saw his face, but he never forgot theirs. Not long afterward, Bobby Joe Ward ended up in a wheelchair for life as a result of an argument with a pimp in Dallas over a girl. Tim Overton was with Bobby Joe when it happened.

"After my transfer to Austin, the first person I look up is Harvey," said Scholl. "Tim is the first name that comes up." Gann brought Scholl up to speed about the disappointing outcome of the TV shop case. The joint investigation on Tim Overton began with that conversation, but it began on a small scale. "Tim was still dealing grass, so we decided that he should be the number one target of our investigation," said Scholl. "We were just relying a whole lot on surveillance—visual surveillance, infiltrating them in an undercover capacity—and informants."

The DPS side of the investigation was entrusted to the narcotics division, with minimal interaction with the Texas Rangers. At the time, according to Scholl, DPS director Homer Garrison had very little confidence in the ranger force.

Informants ran the gamut from violent offenders to gamblers and prostitutes. "Of course, in narcotics, we never did mess with gambling," said Scholl. As members of the vice community, however, gamblers were often pressed into other services. "Gamblers were real good sounding boards," Scholl explained. "Like the drug scene, gambling was pretty well hooked up with a lot of the other scenes, with prostitution, burglary, all that stuff. So we used it as a tool for information."[77]

In the fall of '63, as Sean Connery showed Americans how slick double-zero agents committed government-sanctioned sabotage and murder, Dr. Timothy Leary was spreading the gospel of LSD, and Austin thug culture was still in an old school groove. On the night of Thursday, September 26, five Austin druggie burglars packed up their tools and fanned out over Austin, hitting three different pharmacies with a rough attempt at pinpoint precision.[78]

The APD got the first call at 10:30 p.m. Patrolman Richard Koble noticed a broken window in the back of Renfro-Sommers on West Thirty-fifth Street. The thieves tripped the alarm, rifled the fridge for dope and hauled ass. By that time, the Apothecary Shop on Cameron Road had already been hit.

At a strip mall on Burnet Road, home to a Renfro-Sommers drugstore, Patrolman G.B. Turner heard running footsteps on the rooftop. Too late. Inside, the stars shone through a gaping hole in the ceiling.

Within an hour, Detective Sergeant Tommy M. Olsen found Wayne Jesse James, age twenty-six, nodded out in his car. He had made it all of a few blocks from Renfro-Sommers before succumbing to the urge to tie off and shoot up. Rudely awakened, James was persuaded to snitch on his colleagues.

Olsen called Gann. Warrants were signed. At 2:30 a.m., officers from four different agencies rolled on the French Place neighborhood in East Austin and banged on an apartment door. Darrell Overton, Chester Schutz Jr., Jimmy Wayne von Beiberstein and Morgan Alexander Roberts were all arrested and charged with narcotics and paraphernalia possession.

Chester Schutz, age thirty-five, was an East First Street character and longtime friend of the Overton family. He had done several stints at Huntsville by the time Overton entered junior high. Jimmy von Beiberstein, age twenty-five, was a west side youth with a yen for junk. "Jimmy was tall like a flagpole," said Ernie Scholl. "He's the only guy we ever busted for dealing heroin on a bicycle milk route."

Robert E. Lee "Ernie" Scholl, during his '60s career, worked night and day on surveillance of the Overton/James gang. *Courtesy of Peggy Imbert.*

The drugstore rampage was the lead story in the city section of the *Austin American-Statesman* under a banner headline, "Dope Raid Nets Elite of City's Underworld," as if the Austin equivalent of Al Capone or Mickey Cohen had been taken into custody. Gann was one of several APD officers quoted in the story, but the headline was apparently inspired by the comment of "a veteran officer," who said that the five suspects represented "the cream of Austin's underworld." Because the comment was almost certainly intended as sarcasm, we are left to wonder: did the editors at the *Statesman* have a capricious streak or were they just clueless?

Five days later, a raid on a cabin on Lake Travis netted more dope from the drugstore spree: Dilaudid, sodium pentobarbital, heroin, white powdered substances and a large quantity of pills. The stash of narcotics, later confirmed to have been stolen during the burglaries, was found in an armadillo hole in a bluff behind the cabin.[79]

The signal to commence the bust was the appearance of Tim Overton's Cadillac. Travis County sheriff's deputies came storming out of the cedar breaks. Overton was charged with carrying a sawed-off shotgun. Pills and a pistol were found on his passengers, Darrell Overton and Jimmy von Beiberstein, both recently bailed out of jail, plus a prostitute named Jackie Buck. Also busted were the junkie burglars inside the cabin, John and Vernon Creilia and James Ray Park.

On Halloween night, Darrell Overton was arrested in a downtown building complex at Fifteenth and Lavaca Streets called Rocket Square. Several offices had been broken into, for a total score of seventy dollars. By my count, it was Darrell's fourth arrest on felony charges since July.

Bail was finally arranged on November 19. To celebrate, Darrell and Jimmy von Beiberstein broke into Hyde Park Pharmacy, looted the place for loose pills and were in the process of peeling the safe when the cops arrived, sometime after midnight. Inside Darrell's Volkswagen bus was enough Nembutal Sodium and Dilaudid to sedate a half dozen elephants.

Two days later, on November 22, in Dealey Plaza in Dallas, bullets fired from a Czechoslovakian rifle from a fourth-floor window in the Texas Book Depository Building killed President Kennedy, severely wounded Texas governor John Connally and threw the nation into shock and mourning.[80]

Decades later, many remain unconvinced that Kennedy was killed by Lee Harvey Oswald acting alone. Many alternate theories implicate the mafia in the assassination plot, including specifically Carlos Marcello, the head man in New Orleans. Two well-known fictional accounts, the Oliver Stone film *JFK* and James Ellroy's novel *The Cold Six Thousand*, expound this view, and both of those works were largely adapted from the book *Crossfire: The Plot that Killed Kennedy*, by assassination conspiracy author Jim Marrs. Such narratives commonly implicate the involvement of Dallas organized crime figures such as Joseph Campisi, R.D. Matthews, Charles V. Harrelson and George M. McGann, along with a more complex involvement by Oswald's killer, Jack Ruby, than the official version released by the Warren Commission and other government investigations.

As confirmed by FBI reports from 1964, Tim Overton, Jerry Ray James and Chester Schutz were involved in the same underworld scene in Dallas as those Dallas organized crime figures before and after November 22, 1963.[81]

I don't believe it myself, but if you buy the idea that the Dallas mob played a part in the assassination of JFK, it's not much of a leap to believe that

Overton and his mugs were also involved. A special essay on that topic has been added as an appendix to this book, under the heading "The Overtons in JFK Conspiracyland."

# 3

# CHICKEN SHACK CADILLACS: 1964

*Austin has two other distinctions: a network of 30 towers, 150 feet tall, which bathe the city in fluorescent moonlight, and a house of prostitution in which the hostess, a Negro woman, always seems to be washing collard greens in the sink and the star attraction has a skunk tattooed on each buttock.*[82]
—Time *magazine, 1964*

The sight of Lyndon B. Johnson, a tall, gangly, big-eared Texan, taking the oath aboard Air Force One must have driven the editors of *Time* magazine crazy. The fruit of their frenzied efforts hit the stands eight weeks later. Published on January 17, 1964, *Time* magazine's Texas-themed issue sported a cover banner that said, "Texas: Where Myth & Reality Merge," and a graphic illustration of Governor John B. Connally, looking very **LBJ**-like, with a background of oil rigs, grazing cattle and Houston high-rises. The red border reinforced the message that Texas, home of our new president, killed his beloved predecessor.[83]

Inside was a collection of journalistic essays about **LBJ** and the Lone Star State. Less than half a page was devoted to Texas's major cities. The single paragraph about Austin began and ended on the seedy side of town:

*All of the big cities have large slum areas, occupied mainly by low-income Latins and Negroes—who sometimes feud furiously with each other. Even Austin, the state capital, has its slums but is otherwise a clean-looking city of broad streets, nicely integrated architecture in its state offices, and the*

Lyndon B. Johnson takes the presidential oath on Air Force One, November 22, 1966. *Public domain photo.*

*University of Texas campus. Austin has two other distinctions: a network of 30 towers, 150 feet tall, which bathe the city in fluorescent moonlight, and a house of prostitution in which the hostess, a Negro woman, always seems to be washing collard greens in the sink and the star attraction has a skunk tattooed on each buttock.*

It's a shallow, mean-spirited little blurb, but the description in the middle ("clean-looking city of broad streets, nicely integrated architecture in its state offices, and the University of Texas campus") is a decent verbal postcard view that wisely mentions our moonlight towers.

The "house of prostitution" was M&M Courts, a roadside motel at 8714 South Congress Avenue repurposed as brothel around 1959. Westell, the African American cook mentioned in the article, carried a pistol inside her garter.[84] The owner, Hattie Valdes, was a sixty-year-old white woman, short and stout. In her 1956 mug shot, her eyes are steely, her gaze nonplussed. Her short hair, a white-streaked pompadour, would look just right on a bank president circa 1929—the year when she was prosperous enough to give her attorney, Emmett Shelton, a suite of furniture for his wedding present (unbeknownst to Shelton's future wife).[85]

The "star attraction" at M&M Courts was Judy Cathey. In the county mug book, she's a pretty girl with big, dark hair, a short skirt and white high heels. The expression on her face doesn't give away much. Physical description details were five foot, three inches, 111 pounds, brown eyes and brown hair. "Associates" are listed as "James T. Overton, Jerry Ray James, Dickie Goldstein, Chester Schutz."

Cathey, the girl with the skunk tattoos, was Tim Overton's girlfriend, his number one girl, his own "star attraction." *Time* had just made Overton the most talked-about pimp in town. Making an even better punch line was the rumor that whenever LBJ was in Austin, the hooker he asked for was Judy Cathey, the girl with the skunk tattoos. True or not, Cathey's notoriety undoubtedly inflated Overton's ego, just as the lurid rumor about Cathey and LBJ surely helped sate the JFK-mourning East Coast correspondent's need to denigrate the home state of the thirty-seventh president.

Fortunately, Laylee Muslovik, Judy Cathey's only daughter, generously provided details of her mother's life, few of which have ever been published. A slight digression here might help rescue Cathey from being merely a salacious footnote in a history of Austin's most villainous men.

She was born Judith Ann Lawler on September 8, 1942. Her father, James William "Jim Bill" Lawler, "a petty criminal," was either directly or indirectly responsible for his daughter's initiation into a life of prostitution.

Cathey married Roy Cathey at age fourteen, gave birth to Muslovik and obtained a divorce at age sixteen. Laylee Muslovik, born in 1959, was raised by her paternal grandmother in South Austin, but her mother remained a part of her life throughout her childhood years. Judy contributed financial support, bought clothes and gifts and spent holidays with her.

As for the tattoos, the skunk on the left cheek was a boy, with the name "Ben" inked above it, and on the right was a girl skunk with the name "Judy." The ink was a gift from Judy's previous pimp, Emory Benjamin Curry. Curry was imprisoned on narcotics charges in 1962.[86] Tim Overton took his place.

The daughter of the girl with the skunk tattoos did not like Tim Overton. "I remember when he came into the picture," she said. "He gave me a bad feeling, and I never liked him. When he came to pick Momma up, he never came to the door. He just honked."

Sometimes they took her places. She remembered being in the back seat, pretending to be asleep and smelling "a lot of marijuana smoke."

Overton gave Cathey a mink coat. "It was so pretty," said Muslovik. "She let me touch it. I remember that so well." The memory was underscored by what happened later. "They were arguing and Tim backhanded her. I remember the blood on the mink coat."

Muslovik remembered another time when she walked in the bathroom and Cathey was in the bathtub. "Grandma was washing the blood from Momma's face. I didn't know what being 'pistol-whipped' meant at the time," she told me. "Tim had done that to her."

The worst story: There was an emergency phone call. An uncle came to the house to take Grandma somewhere. "They wanted to leave me home alone, but I threw a fit," she said. "I wouldn't let them. We drove to some apartment. I stayed in the car. When they brought Momma out she was wrapped in a blanket, crying like a baby. Tim had broken both her ankles. That's because she was going to leave him. He told her, 'You're not going to leave me now.'"

*Left and top*: Judy Cathey, November 1962. *Courtesy of Laylee Muslovski.*

After Overton was convicted of conspiracy in 1968 and sent to Leavenworth for five years, Cathey finally left. She tried to quit heroin numerous times without success. She got married again and then divorced and married again. Always, Muslovik said, to "another character." Her last marriage was in 1985 to "the black sheep of a wealthy family." "It was often," Muslovik said, "about the availability of drugs."

Cathey died of a heroin overdose in 1987. Muslovik got married and raised two kids. She says she's come to terms with her mother's legacy and forgiven her failings. With some irony, she says, "Guess what I do for a living? I work for a drug testing company."

When Cathey was Overton's favorite, Sue was still his legal wife. Both women worked for him as prostitutes, as did others, but Cathey remained his most frequent companion. Sometimes he lived with her, sometimes he lived with Sue. In the vice world, the girls were known as "sister-in-laws."

An interview with the two daughters of the former Sue Overton (for the sake of privacy and clarity, they will be referred to as "daughters of Sue Overton") yielded more horror stories of abuse at the hands of Tim Overton. There were times when he threatened them to keep their mother in line. When he left them at his father and stepmother's house, they were tormented by the stepchildren. When they asked for sweet rolls, Overton took them to a Dairy Queen and smashed the sweet rolls in their faces. They also said that their mother required hospitalization from at least one of his beatings.

Prostitution is a dirty business. Stories such as these are sickening reminders of that fact. Tim Overton seems to have been exceptionally abusive. And yet he hid this side of his personality from others. With one exception, his friends told me they never saw any evidence of it. Many, in fact, stressed his positive attributes. They said he was generous and respectful. A number of friends mentioned his desire to protect the weak—which, of course, would seem to be at odds with the characteristic traits of a pimp.

Tim Overton was a celebrity in Austin's fringe community of semi-pro boxers, wrestlers, power-lifters and street fighters. Most were young men who were not lawbreakers, who had excelled in sports in high school and who simply desired to continue exploring new avenues for physical competition. Men like Jesse Woods, Virgil Runnels and Joe Bednarski competed in professional wrestling, boxing exhibitions and circuslike demonstrations of physical strength, such as ripping phone books in half or tearing license plates apart with their teeth. (Runnels competed under the name Dusty Rhodes and Bednarski as "Ivan Putski, the Polish Strongman.")

Like Tim Overton and his friend Don Jester, many were also street fighters. In this community, bare-knuckle fighting was no more unusual or outré than pick-up basketball games or softball. One measure of respect for such men was the number of policemen required to subdue and arrest them. Jesse Woods, who claimed the title "Strongest Man in Austin" in 1976 and was a close friend of Overton in the early '60s, admired Overton so much that he named his first son "James Timothy."[87]

On a rare, quiet afternoon in his law office, located in a historic red brick building at the corner of Guadalupe and Roy Q. Minton Streets, Roy Q. Minton told me about the time Overton gave him a stern lecture for leaving his young female assistant alone at the office with clients in the waiting room, men who were, as Minton described, "mostly good guys who'd gotten into trouble…not hardened criminals like the Overtons." Overton came into his office, shut the door and said, "You've got some of the worst thugs I've ever seen sitting around out there and you walk off and leave her there. I came in and I saw her there and so I sat here and waited till you got back. Don't be leaving here again with that child in here like that."

Janice Farmer, who met Tim Overton in the summer of 1965 and dated his brother John, said she never saw the horrors other women have described. "I never witnessed Tim being abusive," she said. "He always treated me well. He might have treated other women badly, but not in front of me."[88]

WHAT BEGAN AS A MARIJUANA and burglary investigation became a federal case when the task force learned from an informant's tip that the Overtons had been burglarizing small-town banks. Other informants yielded more information, but the tips only came in after the fact. When it came to bank burglary, these wild, outrageous characters were meticulous professionals who erred on the side of caution.

"Luck always seemed to be on their side," said Harvey Gann. "Anything that happened, any good fortune, always seemed to shine on them. Of course, if there was any doubt, if they had any suspicion at all that we were wise to them, all they had to do was blow it off. They seemed to have a knack for that, for knowing that we were watching."

"They cased these jobs way ahead of time," said Scholl. "Some of them they cased years in advance. And they were busy. Just like you and I get up and go to work every day, they were out stealing every day. That was their job."

Proving a conspiracy in federal court was a matter of collecting admissible evidence of a chain of "overt acts" committed by the indicted co-conspirators in furtherance of a crime or, as in this case, what amounted to an ongoing criminal enterprise. Evidence of prostitution, meetings between co-conspirators, buying burglary tools or weapons—all these things would have to be documented, linked together and proven in court. Each element of the case, such as the search warrants under which the incriminating evidence was obtained, would be vigorously challenged in court.

AS THIEVES, THEY WERE NOTHING if not voracious. On January 29, Tim Overton, Jerry Ray James and Hank Bowen went to Abilene for a 3:00 a.m. shopping spree at the Caleb Reed menswear shop. The score, according to the Abilene newspaper, included fifty-two suits and twenty sport coats, valued at $6,000.[89]

By midweek, a tip pointed the investigation toward Austin. Texas Rangers and city dicks hit the streets, rousting the usual suspects and inspecting their suit labels, particularly if they had ties with the Overton gang. Within twelve days, sufficient evidence had been obtained for warrants to be issued for Overton, James and Bowen. The threesome was found at Overton's apartment, handcuffed and chauffeured to Abilene by a Texas Ranger.

Enter John Webster "Webbie" Flanagan, the Overtons' full-service legal representative. So much more than just a criminal defense attorney, Flanagan was from Crystal City, where he made Eagle Scout in the Concho Valley Council in 1939 and served the duration of World War II in the U.S. Marines. He was also an accomplished bush pilot, sued by the State of Texas during the Veterans Land Scandal and obtained his law degree from UT in 1961.[90] Never much of a trial lawyer, he was exquisitely gifted at deal making. According to one story, Flanagan once extorted a large sum of money from political operatives over a sex tape starring then state attorney general Waggoner Carr but failed to deliver the tape, which he claimed he never actually possessed and, as far as he knew, did not exist.[91]

The Caleb Reed case was resolved after Webbie flew to Abilene to meet with the district attorney in Taylor County and negotiated a deal in which the remaining inventory of stolen merchandise was returned in exchange for charges being dismissed. During this same time period, Flanagan stopped by the home of his good friend Billy Brammer, a former aide of LBJ and author of *The Gay Place*, the book that got him fired from that job because of its unflattering fictional portrayal of a Texas politician with a resemblance to LBJ. Dorothy Brown, who was married to Brammer at the time, remembered that Flanagan came to the door and asked if Brammer wanted a pair of alligator shoes. "Billy told Flanagan he would but he couldn't afford things like that," she said. "Flanagan told him, 'Don't worry about it, I've got a whole carload outside.'"[92]

Today, there's not much to see in the 4700 block of Harmon Avenue, an ugly stretch of pavement running parallel to the west side of I-35, unless you're on your way to a nude modeling studio, cheap motel or the Spy Shop, but in 1964, it was the focus of an intense undercover stakeout. A first-floor unit on the north side of a *U*-shaped apartment complex at 4719 Harmon Avenue, called Harmon House, was home to Tim Overton and Hank Bowen.

Hank Bowen was a roommate for a while, and "Fat Jerry" James was a frequent guest. "Jerry Ray was always out there shining his red Cadillac," said Harvey Gann. "He was so proud of that Caddy, I think shining that Caddy that was the only work he ever did."

Betty King and Curt Garrett came down to visit, but not often, she said, because, compared to Overton and James, Garrett was a calm and sober Boy Scout.

"Tim was crazy as a loon," King said. "I liked him, he was funny, he was smart, but you just didn't want to be around him all that much. You couldn't mention anything crazy because he would just go and do it."

"Tim and Jerry were just so funny," said King. "They had the craziest personalities, and that was why you would want to be around them. Everybody teased them, because they were always together. They even fought like a married couple."

Harris Richard "Dickie" Goldstein, age twenty-five, hung out at Harmon House but had a place of his own in Austin. Another star athlete in his high school days, Goldstein now subsidized his heroin habit by serving as a "jigger," or lookout, on bank jobs for the gang.

Chester Arthur "Magoo" Schutz, age thirty-six, with slicked back hair and horn-rimmed glasses, lived in the neighborhood with his girlfriend, Mary Farmer, one of the prettiest of the women who ran with the gang. Schutz met her when she was working at Pop's Pool Hall on South Lamar Boulevard, shortly after her husband was convicted and sentenced to life for the brutal rape of a fifteen-year-old girl. His accomplice in the crime was Farmer's brother. She had a baby and a toddler to care for. She went to work for Schutz as a prostitute and hung out with the gang. They called her Sam.[93]

In the wee hours of the night, Cadillacs would come home to roost at Harmon House, the boys carrying brown paper sacks full of loot and then getting loaded on booze, pot and pills until dawn. Important details were spoken of in code, but occasionally one of them would let something slip, a telling detail or a clue.

In an upstairs apartment in the building directly across from the thugs, other men were listening, hanging on every word. Ernie Scholl was one of the eavesdroppers. His colleagues were DPS or APD. The apartment manager, a retired United States Air Force sergeant, was happy to do his part.

"He spread a rumor that we were all gay," said Scholl. No one bothered them.

Microphones and transmitters powered by C-cell batteries were covertly installed in certain furnishings. The task force also relied on informants, visual surveillance and an array of quasi-legal tricks. Information gleaned from the bugs was not admissible in court and could only be used for intelligence gathering. Scholl claimed that they didn't even keep written notes.

Scholl had a gift for blending in, standing in the shadows. He was the guy hugging the wall at Ernie's Chicken Shack, nursing the same drink all night, as Overton and the boys dug the sounds of Blues Boy and the Jets and threw money around.

The shack was at 1167 Webberville Road, deep East Austin and mojo heavy.[94] It served fried chicken, set-ups, half-pints of whiskey in a brown bag and afterhours blues. B.B. King, Bobby Blue Bland, Joe Tex, Freddie King and other big name recording artists popped up in the corner with the band when they were in town. W.C. Clark played bass for a time. Soaking up the vibes in the crowd were young white guys who later helped establish Austin as a music mecca—Paul Ray, Denny Freeman, Doyle Bramhall and others.

When the owner, Ernest Charles Gildon, changed the name of the bar from Cheryl Ann's to Ernie's Chicken Shack, he was sending a message to the black community, his neighbors. That was 1960, in deep East Austin. In Chicago in the 1930s, Ernie's Chicken Shack was one of the Windy City's most popular, most talked-about nightspots. The owner, Ernie Henderson, was one of the most famous black celebrities in the United States. A fleet of red delivery cars with huge roosters on the sides delivered chicken sandwiches all over Chicago's South Side and in white neighborhoods, too. Black pride, 1930s style, Henderson was a character who had hustled his way to the top and wanted everybody to know it. He rode in a bowtie Duesenberg, attended by a chauffeur and footman. His closet held one hundred suits. He was the best-dressed man in America, he said of himself, a line that the press obligingly repeated.[95]

Ernest Charlie Gildon of Austin was a pistol-packing, dice-shooting character himself. Gildon's other music club, Charlie's Playhouse, was at 1206 East Eleventh Street. Unfortunately, Charlie's had a Caucasian problem. White UT students called early to book up all the tables, preventing black residents of the neighborhood from partaking in their own culture. Yet blacks were still barred from such places on the west (white) side of town.

Gildon already owned Cheryl Ann's before 1960. Changing the name and serving fried chicken, just like Ernie's Chicken Shack in Chicago in the 1930s, was Gildon's overture to address the problem. Certain illicit delights were probably common to both venues. The shack wasn't exactly exclusive to African Americans, but the clientele was considerably blacker than Charlie's or the I.L. Club, the competition catty-corner to it on East Eleventh Street.[96]

Gildon made sure that characters like Tim Overton got a good table. "It was professional courtesy," said Charles Schotz, "from one character to another."

One night when the floor was a den of alligator hide and two-tone Stacy Adams shoes, Charles Schotz edged inside looking for a seat that wasn't taken, and Tim Overton waved him over.

Overton said to him, "Hey man, how you doing? You want one of these girls?"

Schotz said, "No thanks, Tim. I've got a girlfriend."

"You sure? Pick anyone you want, even this one next to me."

"No thanks, really, I'm fine."

"How about some money, you need some money? Here, here's a hundred bucks, you can catch me on the back side."

Schotz really liked Tim Overton. "He was generous," he said. "That was one of his attributes."

ED WENDLER OFTEN WATCHED THE outlaws gather at the Iron Gate Inn, a downtown bar located at 1101 Trinity. "It was fascinating, watching them make an entrance," said Wendler. "There would always be five or six of them and several women. They would file in, and you could see a couple of them come in first, scouting the place. Then Tim would come in with the women."

Past the midnight hour, the place would fill up with more characters: car dealers, pimps, burglars, fixers and strong-armers. Overton always sat with his back to the wall, "just like in the movies." Either intimidated or offended, some of the regulars would leave. But the Overtons "never bothered anybody."

"They were just as nice and quiet and gentlemanly as you could be."

HATTIE VALDES WOULD TELL YOU that the Overtons were not always gentlemen. Late on Friday night, April 3, she drove home in her pink Cadillac. The weather was nice, so she probably wasn't wearing her mink coat, but she likely had lots of jewelry on, as usual. She turned down her driveway at 403 East Riverside Drive, where she lived in a two-story bungalow on the edge

The former Hattie Valdes residence, 403 East Riverside Drive, much changed but it still has a multimillion-dollar view. *Author's collection.*

of a high bluff. From her windows, she had a commanding view of Town Lake, downtown and many of the parts of town where she owned valuable commercial and residential real estate.

She parked the Caddy in the carport and let herself in. Three masked men were waiting. Two wore ski masks; the other had a custom-made leather hood. They had entered from a hole cut into the floor from the bluff.[97]

The robbers demanded $25,000. She said she didn't have it. They tied her to a chair and beat her. She told police later that she said, "You can't get blood out of a turnip."

The paper cited Hattie's statements to police that the robbers got only $2,000 in cash and $5,500 in jewelry, which was most likely an understatement, for a number of reasons that would be obvious to someone in a similar business.

Like others in her position, Hattie had been robbed many times before, but it wasn't always mentioned in the press. According to the *Statesman*, she told the police she had no idea who the robbers were. But that wasn't true. She knew that Tim and James were the men behind the masks. Why didn't she tell the police?

As Betty King explained, the relationship between the Overtons and the vice world in Austin might be too nuanced for an outsider to understand. "Tim Overton robbed Hattie so many goddamn times, and he just loved her," she said.

Fat Jerry loved her, too, as King observed one night after the robbery, when she happened to be visiting Hattie in the front lobby of M&M Courts.

"I was out there at the motel," she said, "and Jerry came in and Hattie said, 'I don't know why you had to do that, Jerry, I don't know why you had to beat me up.' He said, 'Well, it was just business. You know I love you.' So, that's the kind of person Jerry was."

IN THE EARLY MORNING HOURS of Sunday, November 8, burglars hit Citizens State Bank in Kyle, a small town on I-35 twenty-two miles south of Austin. After peeling the doorframe off the vault to access the safe, the thieves worked on the safe but failed to get it open. They did get away with $500 in paper currency that had been stored outside the safe, plus an estimated $2,000 in coins. Using a device called a "nose-puller," the burglars opened all the safe deposit boxes, dumped the contents into a pile on the floor and sifted out the valuables.

Scholl and Gann had suspicions but no evidence. In 1968, Overton's stepmother, Florine Craine, told a packed courtroom that she was awakened one Sunday morning by Overton and James, who were counting out the loot from the bank job in her living room. Later that day, she found a bank bag labeled "Citizens State Bank, Kyle, Texas." She burned the bag and flushed the ashes down the toilet.[98]

The modus operandi of the Kyle caper fit the Overton gang to a T. Kyle was a rural town, population one thousand.[99] It was not a county seat, and therefore, there was no sheriff's office in town. There was no city police force, only a night watchman.

The next bank job, on December 10, also fit the pattern. The National Bank of Oglesby was burglarized using the same methods. The safe was not penetrated. Oglesby is about one hundred miles northwest of Austin. The population today is 452, and the town covers about five-tenths of a mile.[100] Although the evidence was sketchy, the task force added Oglesby to the list of bank burglaries attributed to the gang. By the time the case went to court, there would be close to thirty banks on the list.

Between Kyle and Oglesby came one heist that was completely outside the pattern, and yet in hindsight, the task force should have been there waiting. It was perfect.

On Thanksgiving Day, November 25, 1964, President Johnson and Lady Bird were at the Johnson ranch in Stonewall, keeping dinner warm while Luci and Lynda were at Memorial Stadium in a sell-out crowd of 65,700, cheering the Longhorns to victory. Ranked number five in the nation, Texas was a fourteen-point favorite to win. A *Statesman* front-page photo shows Luci in the stands, her mouth open as wide as the *o* in Johnson.

For Texas college football fans, the Texas/A&M game was almost as important a part of Thanksgiving Day as the turkey dinner. Scholl and Gann had other concerns. From the tempo of activity at the Harmon Avenue apartment, they could tell that something was planned, but they didn't know what.

Unlike Austin in 2015, when almost every weekend sees a marathon race, a music festival and other gridlock-inducing events, Austin in 1964 braced for a big football game like a little country town before the annual Watermelon Thump or rodeo week. The *Statesman* crowed that the Texas/A&M game would bring an extra nineteen thousand automobiles into town, which siphoned off fifty to sixty city policemen to handle traffic. It almost sounded like an open invitation to thieves.[101]

Tickets were sold at the UT Co-op, the college bookstore on the Drag. The store also cashed checks for students and faculty. By closing time on Wednesday, the safe was stuffed with cash like a Thanksgiving turkey.

Campus was deserted, as there were no classes until Monday. Nothing was open. Dormitories had emptied out. The night turned cold and rainy.

Detectives Ernie Scholl and Tommy Olsen were on surveillance. Overton and James went out early. Following them wasn't practical, and the thugs would have spotted them anyway. The boys came home about 2:30 a.m.

*Time* magazine, January 17, 1964. The Texas-themed issue mentioned a brothel and Tim's prostitute girlfriend and her skunk tattoos. Classy. *Author's collection.*

"We're listening on one of our makeshift bugs, and we can tell they've pulled something," said Scholl. "We hear them start cutting it up. They're counting the money, and we hear them count out over twenty-some-odd thousand dollars. I called Harvey, and he called the burglary lieutenant and told him to get his people out on the ground. We had to find out where this money came from."

They worked the phones but didn't find out anything until Friday morning. When the assistant manager of the UT Co-op came to open the store at 8:00 a.m., he found the place in shambles. Burglars had bypassed the alarm and then jimmied the back door. They entered the walk-in vault by punching the combination lock, which set off the tear gas bomb. The gas apparently temporarily halted the burglars, as evidenced by the puddles of vomit on the floor. Ever resourceful, the burglars commandeered an electric fan from a downstairs window display to clear the fumes.

The safe was a steel box, four feet wide and four feet tall. The burglars used an electric grinder to expose end layers of laminate and then used a short-handled sledge and chisel to peel the layers like an onion, finally producing a gaping hole.

Investigators said it was obviously the work of professionals. The *Statesman* report referred to them as "yeggs," an archaic term no longer in common use. Co-op management refused to divulge the total amount of the loss. The *Statesman* cited "veteran criminal investigators" who "could not recall an Austin safe burglary to match the figure mentioned in the Thanksgiving holiday strike."[102]

Ernie Scholl and Harvey Gann's team knew that Tim Overton, Jerry Ray James, Chester Schutz and Dickie Goldstein had knocked over the Co-Op, but there was nothing they could do about it.

A week later, Overton, James and Schutz appeared on the new car lot at the Charles Maund Cadillac dealership. Overton and James paid cash for new Cadillacs. Schutz got a souped-up, late model T-Bird. The cash came from brown paper sacks. Goldstein, the jigger, had been paid a much smaller split. He bought a '59 Plymouth from the retired DPS highway patrol fleet.

On Thanksgiving Day 1964, Texas defeated A&M 26–7, but Tim Overton stole the Thanksgiving turkey right off of Darrell Royal's dinner table.

# 4
# CRIME WAVE: 1965

The Federal Highway Act of 1956 transformed the physical face of the nation. As far-flung points on the national map were linked together, the concept of distance seemed to shrink, creating the kind of connectivity we now associate with the Internet. The interstate highway system was also a boon to traveling criminals.

The list of thirteen bank burglaries attributed to the Overton gang in 1965 alone shows that they were heavy users of the I-35 corridor between Texas, Oklahoma, Kansas and Missouri.

Evant, Texas, January 25
Kosse, Texas, March 5[103]
Iredell, Texas, April 3
Oxford, Kansas, April 25
Pflugerville, Texas, June 5
Emory, Texas, June 17
Oregon, Missouri, November 4
Meriden, Kansas, November 7
Alta Vista, Kansas, November 11
Roxbury, Kansas, November 23
St. Paul, Kansas, December 16
Lucas, Kansas, December 29
Coupland, Texas, December 27[104]

Each of these towns fit the gang's modus operandi: population fewer than one thousand, not a county seat and no city police force. Evant, Kosse and Iredell were West Texas towns less than an hour's drive from Waco. From Austin to Waco was a quick trip north on I-35. Another factor was the abundance of Holiday Inns, their preferred motor hotel.

In a typical heist scenario, some of the burglars would leave from Austin and rendezvous with the rest of the team in a designated place. They usually took separate cars. Tim Overton and Jerry Ray James were always the team captains, with the inside team usually consisting of one additional man. The fourth, the jigger, remained outside with a walkie-talkie.

The bank cases brought down the wrath and resources of the Federal Department of Justice. Title 18 of the United States' criminal code covers stealing money from a bank insured by the Federal Deposit Insurance Corporation (FDIC), whether through threat of violence or by burglary. Each act—breaking in with intent to steal, taking the money with you and taking it across state lines—meant incurring another offense.

Under Title 18 of the federal criminal code, a car dealer, a prostitute or anyone else who met with one of the other conspirators to discuss burglarizing a bank (even if the plan was never executed) or committed any other "overt act" that assisted the conspiracy could be charged with being a co-conspirator.

Federal conspiracy laws were written in such a way that the prosecutor's side had the advantage over the accused in court. That was fortunate for the government because, the way things were going, the boys would never be caught in the act of burglarizing a bank.

But those things only mattered once the case had been glued together sufficiently enough to try it in the federal courts. Despite any great home field advantages for the government in the courtroom, Ernie Scholl, Harvey Gann and their colleagues on the task force still faced enormous problems pulling the case together in a way that could obtain convictions. In many respects, as late as 1964 and '65, the investigation was still out in the weeds. Forensic evidence was painstakingly studied, but in most instances, the

*Opposite, top*: This is believed to be the First National Bank in Evant, Texas, hit by the gang on January 25, 1965. *Courtesy of the NARA.*

*Opposite, bottom*: Probably the First National Bank of Lucas, Kansas. On December 29, 1965, the burglars peeled the vault door from the frame and looted the safety deposit boxes. *Courtesy of the NARA.*

burglars had been careful and efficient. Sometimes they left tools behind, but they never left fingerprints. Their lives were crazy and messy, but when they plotted and executed a bank job, they were cautious professionals and took few chances.

Informants were being cultivated, but reliability was always a big question. To briefly flash forward to the 1968 conspiracy trial: Richard Hinton was one of many used car dealers and part-time burglars who ran errands for Overton. As a government witness, Hinton testified that Overton often bragged to him about his latest heists. Hinton testified that on June 10, 1965, at Snooks Overton's house on Goodwin Avenue, Overton retrieved a paper sack containing $5,500 in cash from a hidden compartment in the attic and sent him to purchase a Cadillac he had already picked out, giving specific orders on how to fill out the vehicle registration so it couldn't be traced back to him.[105]

In the twelve months prior to the trial, Hinton had been convicted on a multitude of felony charges, including bank burglary and conviction as a habitual criminal. Going through my own case files, it's a little hard to find a major burglary in Austin in which Hinton was not involved and did not eventually snitch out his partners.

> *Objects of the Conspiracy: Object No. 13*
> *Throughout* [March 13, 1964 to about April 20, 1966], *the evidence warrants a finding that the Overton Transmission Exchange served as a headquarters for the above operations…Burglary tools such as crow bars, punches and a magnetic drill as well as a good deal of black clothing, several pairs of rubber soled shoes and gloves were kept there. In addition, the evidence also reveals that a safe, similar to those in which banks kept their currency, was, for a period of time, also kept there and various members of the gang utilized the above and other tools in an attempt to learn how to penetrate it.*[106]

In his opening statement in the 1968 conspiracy trial, United States attorney Ernest Morgan alleged that the Transmission Exchange had served

*Opposite, top*: The burglars used an acetylene torch to enter the vault at the First National Bank in Evant, Texas. *Courtesy of the NARA.*

*Opposite, bottom*: The burglars sometimes used a magnesium torch, but only rarely—the heat (seven thousand degrees) could easily burn up the contents of the safe. *Courtesy of the NARA.*

the gang as, among other things, a "crime school." Evidence supporting that claim was referred to in the section of the indictment listing the objects of the conspiracy.

The safe referred to in the indictment was a second-hand Mosler cylindrical, commonly called a "cannonball." The basic design dated to the 1800s, but most cannonball safes found in banks in the 1960s were probably made by Mosler in the early 1900s. They were made of Mangalloy, a manganese-carbon steel alloy that was non-magnetic and highly resistant to abrasion. Superior lock mechanisms and massive hinges, combined with the absence of right angles (which made attaching hooks and cables nearly impossible), made cannonball safes extremely difficult to open using rudimentary safecracking techniques. This was the reason Tim Overton bought one—so he could study and learn its weaknesses.[107]

Overton purchased the second-hand cannonball in late 1964 or early 1965 and sent the shop foreman, James W. Lloyd, to Houston, using the wrecker to bring it back to Transmission Exchange. Three Overton brothers—Tim, Darrell and Charles Ray—tried opening it using drills, grinders and acetylene torches. Lloyd gave it a shot himself. He told the FBI that none of their efforts was successful. Sometime in early 1965, he drove the thing to a cow pasture near Elgin and dumped it.[108]

Lloyd had worked for Snooks Overton since 1954, when the shop was located on East Sixth Street. In a later era, the building served as part of the punk rock venue Emo's.

The shop foreman bitterly disapproved of the garage being transformed into a front for an underworld gang, or at least, he came off that way when he was in the company of FBI agents and when testifying as a witness for the prosecution regarding his role as an unindicted co-conspirator. Lloyd resented the fact that Overton had given Snooks $15,000 cash from a heist to become half owner of the business, and afterward, profits for the shop declined precipitously. Valuable shop equipment disappeared, including two welding rigs in 1965 alone (under normal use, he said, such equipment could last ten years or so), and he hated to see $600 spent on a magnetic drill—a heavy-duty portable drill with an electromagnetic armature—a tool that could be quite effective in drilling safes "but had absolutely no use in the shop."

ONCE IT WAS DETERMINED THAT the United States attorney needed evidence of prostitution activity in conjunction with the conspiracy, laws against sex for hire were rigidly enforced in areas where the law had previously been more conspicuous for having its hand out and eyes averted. Country town bordellos, places that the Overton gang depended on for steady income, were suddenly being raided.

One January morning in 1965, Ernie Scholl and Jack Carpenter left Austin around midnight and broke a few speed limits in order to arrive at the Ware Hotel in Plainview around dawn. Scholl and Carpenter entered the lobby, flashed their badges at the desk clerk and said, "You're gonna take us to the room where the whores are and knock on the door without any advance warning." The desk clerk feigned surprise. As Scholl remembered it, the clerk seemed to have attempted to paraphrase Claude Raines in one of the brilliant scenes in the film *Casablanca*, saying something like, "I'm shocked, SHOCKED…to hear it suggested that there is prostitution in this hotel!"

Judy Cathey, Mary Farmer and Sue Overton were taken into custody, booked and put on the next Greyhound bus back to Austin.

"The police captain there was a sharpie who wore silk shirts and alligator shoes," said Scholl, "and the rest of them were a bunch of klutzes. He resigned the next day." If the exact details as Scholl recalled them were slightly different, the basic scenario was as old as time itself.

"We went up there and sacked those whores up, because as long as those prostitutes are up there, sending them money, Tim and them were just laying around," said Scholl. "It was just a little maneuver to get these guys going again. We wanted them to hit the bricks."

Plainview was one of more than a dozen stops on the prostitution circuit. Most were country towns. San Antonio was an anomaly. Lubbock was bigger than most. Besides Plainview, there were Abilene, Amarillo, Kilgore, La Grange, McCamey, Midland, Mineral Wells, Odessa,

Judy Cathey. *Courtesy of Laylee Muslovski.*

Pampa, Sweetwater, Tyler and Waco. And there were places in New Mexico, Oklahoma, Louisiana and Mississippi. When Tim Overton was arrested in 1966, police confiscated two address books filled with names, places and average weekly income. The names of the venues alone sound like the titles of blues albums.

The circuit became especially important to Tim Overton after Hattie Valdes banned his girls from her bordello sometime in 1964. The exact reason for the ban isn't clear, but tying her up, beating and robbing her couldn't have helped the relationship. George O. Jackson said that Hattie was never personally fond of Judy Cathey. When I asked Jackson if he could think of any other reason Hattie refused to let Overton's girls work for her, he said, "You know, I think Hattie might have done it because Tim was always beating her up (meaning Judy)."[109]

The ban might have been someone else's idea. Truth was, Hattie enjoyed a mostly friendly relationship with law enforcement, and if Harvey Gann, Ernie Scholl or Sheriff T.O. Lang told her to embargo women who worked for certain mutually disliked local crime figures, she probably would have been happy to do so.

On April 25, 1965, Tim Overton, Jerry Ray James, Benjamin Thomas Tisdale and Chester Schutz broke into the First State Bank in Oxford, Kansas. An FBI report put the amount stolen at $28,251. On most bank jobs, after breaking into the vault, two of the men worked on the safe while the third opened the safety deposit boxes and sacked up any cash and negotiable instruments stored in the vault. The take from the safety deposit boxes often included valuable jewels, coin collections and traveler's checks. The gang had a mafia connection in Chicago named Joseph Spagnoli who paid cash for traveler's checks.[110]

Ben Tisdale was still driving his '52 Oldsmobile on the Oxford job. On April 28, Tisdale and Bowen drove to Oklahoma to visit Harley Clowe, their friendly Cadillac dealer in Chickasha. Bowen bought a Cadillac. Tisdale paid $5,900 for a 1965 Cadillac with low mileage. The next day, Tisdale and his girlfriend, Elizabeth Agnes Sherman, went back to the dealer and bought another '65 Cadillac just like the first one but had the title assigned to Sherman. Jerry Ray James bought two Cadillacs from Harry Clowe, too, and the dealer was happy to pretend that James was a person named Jerome B. Jennings, even though he had sold cars to James before when his name was something else. In the 1968 trial, the government would offer up vehicle purchases such as these, listing each one as a separate act committed in furtherance of the conspiracy.

AROUND MAY 15, 1965, ACTING on solid leads, Ernie Scholl and Harvey Gann rolled out of Austin heading north. At the Big Tex steakhouse in Amarillo, they met up with several DPS detectives and then continued to their destination, Walsenburg, a town in southeastern Colorado. The agents actually arrived ahead of their surveillance subjects, Tim Overton, Jerry Ray James, Ben Tisdale, Hank Bowen and Chester Schutz, plus their respective girlfriends. All the men drove new vehicles with big V-8 engines: Overton, a '65 Cadillac; James, a '65 Cadillac; Bowen, a '65 Pontiac; Schutz, a '64 Thunderbird; and Tisdale, a '65 Oldsmobile. Elizabeth Sherman drove a '62 Plymouth.

The thugs arrived and checked in at a motel. Ernie Scholl, disguised as a desk clerk, assigned the rooms, each of which had already been wired with eavesdropping devices. One of the gang's main connections in town was George Stanford, better known in underworld circles as Joe Swift. Swift had a '64 Cadillac and a '52 Plymouth. For the next three days, Overton and the boys cased banks and other targets. They held conferences with Swift and other local gamblers and characters. Texas detectives and Colorado troopers maintained close surveillance.

On the fourth day, Overton hurriedly drove Judy Cathey to a hospital in the town of Pueblo. She'd suffered a miscarriage.[111] Following Cathey's release from the hospital, all the Texans—cops and outlaws both—drove home.

DEBI DABBS REMEMBERED TRAVELING A lot with her mother and her mother's boyfriend at an early age from Chicago to New Orleans, Houston, Austin, Odessa, Tennessee, Oklahoma City and so on. It was a strange, fast-moving life.

"It was fun," she told me. "It seemed normal at the time. It was exciting. You know that movie *Casino*? It was kind of like that. And now, when I remember all the FBI men and their big cars pulling up to the house to talk to us, it makes me think of *Men in Black*. All those black cars and men in suits, it's funny when I think about it now."

Dabbs had just turned six when Jerry Ray James called her mom and said to pack up everything in a U-Haul and meet him in Texas. Dabbs's mother was Betty Joyce Dabbs, twenty-three, a youthful-looking, chameleon-like beauty, a prostitute and sometimes dancer from Savannah, Tennessee. She had more aliases than all the guys in the gang combined. The 1968 conspiracy indictment listed her as Joan Dobbs Taylor. Hattie knew her as Joyce. Most of the detectives and lawyers I interviewed called her Joan or Joanie. The name Dobbs, with an *o*, seems to have originated as a typo.

James called her Joan, but she signed at least half of her correspondence with him as Betty.

Let's call her Joan Taylor for now.

Joan was living in an apartment in New Orleans in early 1965 with a man named George Romei. She met Jerry James at a party in April. He asked her to dye his hair blond, which she did. A few days later, he came back and said that he needed to have a talk with Romei. The two men left together. When James came back, he moved his stuff into the apartment. Romei never came back.

Because he was dead.[112]

Webbie Flanagan had a place for James, Taylor and Dabbs out in West Lake Hills, a community in the hills on the western fringe of Austin. The

The Red Carpet Club in Biloxi was robbed on March 25, 1966, by Jerry Ray James and five others. James got three years, I got two chips. *Author's collection.*

area was more rural and quiet than the city, and it was close to the Highland Lakes on the Colorado River. The three-bedroom house on Reveille Road also had ample room for storing hot merchandise—everything from collectible guns to antique clocks, menswear, cases of cigarettes, razor blades and chewing gum.

"There was a lot going on there, all the time," Dabbs said. "And for some reason, I was only allowed in the back yard one time, but I remember it was like being out in the woods." Flanagan had leased the house to the couple under the names John and Nan Wolf, as in "Little Red Riding Hood."

"We had two boats," said Dabbs. "There was a little speedboat and a big one called *Sea Witch*." In late April, there was a James family reunion. Everyone went out to Lake Travis for water skiing and picnicking.[113] Flanagan and his wife also accompanied them on boat outings and at least once, Dabbs said, went with them to Six Flags.

Two weeks before meeting Taylor, on the night of March 25, 1965, James and four other men had robbed the Red Carpet Club, a gambling casino on the Highway 90 strip in Biloxi, Mississippi. Heavyweight Dixie Mafia guys owned the club. Harry Bennett and Dewey DeAngelo, the two front men, had been indicted by a federal grand jury earlier in the week for running a "juice joint," a place where an electromagnetic device had been installed under the roulette table and the play could be controlled by means of a hidden switch. Bennett was currently underwater in debt and would be gunned down on December 16, 1967, on the strip near his club.

The robbers got away from the casino with $11,000. Later, in his defense, James told a judge that it was only $3,600, and the blackjack dealer had unfairly cheated him out of that precise amount on the night of the robbery. By the time James decided to move to Texas with Taylor, the other suspects had been apprehended and arraigned on charges.

Jerry Ray James had a number of criminal cases that were overdue for attention. Webbie Flanagan made arrangements and started collecting fees. James met with Flanagan in Houston, where he surrendered on the Red Carpet charges, posted bond and, after his release, tended to some illegal business opportunities with Tim Overton.

Meanwhile, Ernie Scholl was following these developments by eavesdropping on Overton and Bowen's apartment on Harmon Avenue.

"Tim kept getting these calls from Frenchie Dubroc," said Scholl. Dubroc was one of the Red Carpet triggermen and a frequent partner in crime with the Overton/James group. "Frenchie had been following this bookie from New Orleans, who had a lot of money on him, and he followed him all the

Betty Joyce Dabbs with her daughter, Debi Dabbs, 1964. FBI and Overton/James gang task force officers called her Joan Dobbs Taylor. *Courtesy of Debi Dabbs.*

way to Houston."[114] Overton and James drove down to Houston, where they met up with Dubroc and robbed the bookie of $60,000.

Other than the boat trips, the swirl of activity at the house on Reveille Road and the rooms filling up with swag, Debi Dabbs has one other powerful memory about Austin. "We were driving on the interstate and I remember when the blue lights came on," said Debi. "It was the last time Mama was arrested and taken to the police station in Austin. We had a standard drill, because I remember asking her, 'Mama, what's my name tonight?' I don't remember what it was that night, but it might have been Dee Dee. She said her name was Anne Taylor, and I think that's what they booked her under. Later on it was Joyce, but most people called her Joan. She was Mama to me, so I didn't care. I didn't think anything about it."

# 5

# BUGGING OUT: 1965

As the '60s reached their midpoint, there was a buzz in the air, and it wasn't just methamphetamine paranoia or the news that the great folk messiah, Bob Dylan, had gone electric. Young Austinites found common ground over progressive politics, perpetual sunshine, world-class swimming holes, cheap Mexican pot and music. Almost everybody cool smoked pot, and in Texas, one reefer could get you ten years in the joint.[115] Most drug lawyers at that time were also part of the progressive community and, thus, were the attorneys you called if you got arrested at a peace march or a stand-in at a movie theater or café that refused to serve African Americans.

One of the brightest of the bunch was Brooks Holman. Holman also represented Tim Overton on civil rights cases. Not every time Overton entered a courtroom was he trying to avoid going to jail.

THE THUGS MOVED OUT OF Harmon House in May. Hank Bowen rented a new place under the name Clifford B. Linker but spent most of his time in the gambling joints between Omaha, Nebraska, and Council Bluffs, Iowa, often in conjunction with Curt Garrett and Ben Tisdale.[116]

Overton moved into a duplex at 3314 Westhill Drive, just before it terminates at Barton Creek. Flanagan was his landlord. Unbeknownst to either of them, the tenants in the adjoining unit were police informants.[117] A private detective named R.C. Hullum, wearing a utility company uniform, installed a microphone inside Overton's wall heater, connecting it to a battery and transmitter in a closet in the adjoining unit. The task force monitored

The armored vaults of small-town banks often held a variety of so-called safety deposit boxes, including fishing tackle boxes. The contents were sometimes quite valuable. *Courtesy of the NARA.*

the bug from a nearby residence and made regular visits to the apartment to replace the battery and check in with the tenants there, Susanne Ely and Catherine Wilson.

Late on Friday night, June 4, Overton got a call from Jerry James, and Ernie Scholl was listening. The rogue Odessan wanted to do something, but a rainstorm was in progress. The bridge between West Lake Hills and Austin was flooding. Only a fool would risk trying to cross over to Austin.[118]

When the going got tough, the thugs somehow got going. The next day, Scholl learned that burglars had hit the First State Bank of Pflugerville. Pflugerville fit the modus operandi: population 450, fifteen miles north of Austin, not a county seat and no police force.[119]

Later investigation revealed the identities of the burglars: Tim Overton, Jerry Ray James, Chester Schutz, Hank Bowen and Dickie Goldstein. State agents made a report on their methods later that afternoon. The burglars had trouble punching the lock on the vault door. After several attempts to defeat the relocking mechanism, they blew it off and peeled the doorframe. Inside they found 125 fishing tackle boxes secured with padlocks, containers that the bank preferred to call "safe deposit boxes." These were quickly opened with bolt cutters and relieved of their contents. A coin collection later netted them $10,000. They worked on the safe a bit, but it was getting late, and they blew it off. The next day, a neighbor told police he remembered hearing men laughing and joking.

ON JUNE 10, OVERTON DISCOVERED the bug in the wall heater. The timing of arrest reports (vagrancy and drunkenness) suggests that he raised hell about it. After being released on bail, Overton met with attorney Brooks Holman, who suggested filing a civil rights suit in federal court against Lieutenant Harvey Gann and other police officials. Overton liked the idea. Holman began drawing up papers.[120]

Overton moved in with his brother John, the straight-and-narrow college student.[121] They spent a lot of time together after hours and were regular customers at Austin's coolest new go-go discotheque, Le Lollypop.

Le Lollypop was a private club at a swank new apartment complex at 1818 Lakeshore Drive. The club offered mixed drinks, go-go dancers and a live band on Friday nights, plus access to a putting green, a swimming pool and tennis courts, all this for a nominal membership fee. To get around the state ban on liquor-by-the-drink, establishments like the Club Caravan (at the Villa Capri motor lodge, one of Austin's most prestigious music rooms of the '60s) operated as "private clubs" and were thus allowed to serve mixed drinks or set-ups for membership fees as low as ten dollars a year.[122]

Janice Farmer was eighteen years old when she started dancing at the club. During a break, she met Tim and John Overton. She and John started dating.

"I was just this cute kid and John and I were just having fun together," said Janice. "I didn't have a clue who his family was. Then I started reading the newspaper and thinking, holy cow, I'm hanging out with a pretty rough group of people."

Hattie Valdes also frequented the club, but Farmer had no idea who she was. Farmer was still living at home with her parents. Her father, Joe Farmer, was a professional musician in a country-western band. Neither parent knew that she was go-go dancing. One day, writing in his entertainment column in the *Statesman*, John Bustin touted Janice Farmer as one of the new attractions at Le Lollypop.

"Wham, there was my name," she said. "My father told me to quit or move out. I moved out."

John was a nice guy, she said, and was serious about college. Farmer never saw Overton being abusive toward women, she said. If anything, he adopted a paternal attitude toward her. "One time I was over at Tim's place, and he said, 'Janice, you need to stop dating John, you just need to get out of this.' I think he knew how innocent I was and didn't want anything to happen to me."

"It was fun," she said. "We didn't wait tables, we just danced. And after we danced we'd go back in the dressing room and just hang out, so we didn't interact with any of the customers, not while we were working."

After her shift at Le Lollypop, Farmer would drive over to the brothers' house, and they'd all go out to Ernie's Chicken Shack to eat and then dance some more.

"I was just an innocent bystander," she said. "We were having a great time. I didn't understand the danger I was in. One night after work I was driving Tim's car and the police were following me on the way to his house.

I was so stupid, I said, 'Well, sure, if you want to search the car, go ahead,' not realizing all the stuff that was in the car.

"I came home one time and these police are searching my apartment. I can't believe I didn't get arrested. I didn't freak out about it because, well, it just happened."

An arsonist set fire to the go-go club in early 1966. The club was destroyed, but the apartment complex at 1818 Lakeshore Drive survives as a gated condominium complex called the Waterfront.

Tim Overton's civil rights suit sought a permanent injunction on the use of electronic surveillance and $35,000 in damages against two city detectives, Lieutenant Harvey Gann and Major Knox R. Herbert (Herbert was the Austin Police Department's chief of detectives), and the next-door tenants, Susanne Ely and Catherine Wilson.[123]

The petition accused the defendants of violating Tim Overton's rights to equal protection under the law, citing the Fourth, Ninth and Fourteenth Amendments in the Bill of Rights. Overton's anti-bugging suit was not unlike the anti-surveillance cases now common in the post-9/11 world. The technology was more primitive, but the constitutional issues are little changed.

The public first heard about the case on Friday, July 16, 1965. Tim Overton was all over the front page.[124] The banner headline looked like a PR victory—"U.S. Court Suit Charges His Home 'Bugged'"—as did the subhead above the two-column story on the right side of the page, "Tim Overton Claims Civil Rights Violated." Overton was identified as "a known police character," with four paragraphs devoted to his criminal history.

Readers were probably more interested in the boxed article in the middle of the front page, under the eye-grabbing headline "Gangsterism—Austin-Style: One Night at Hattie's."[125]

*Buried deep in the confidential files of Austin and Travis County law enforcement officers there is mounting evidence of tough hoodlums and gangsterism—Chicago style.*

*The latest incident was hidden in sheriff's officers' accounts of the arrest last weekend of six men and three women at the M&M Courts, an outwardly shabby cluster of cabins outside the city limits on South Congress Avenue…*

*In addition to Hattie Valdes, the long-time patroness of Austin prostitution, the key figures involved included two men who rank first and third on the Austin police confidential list of the city's most notorious thugs.*

The police action described in "Gangsterism" was not a terribly complicated scenario. In the early morning hours of Saturday, July 10, 1966, Tim Overton and Jerry Ray James showed up at M&M Courts, armed with sawed-off shotguns. It's unclear whether they had friends with them or not, but they probably did.

There was no element of surprise. Overton's desire to take over the sex trade in Austin was one of the worst kept secrets in town, but Hattie Valdes had also been tipped to the fact that Overton and James had planned to make a move on her by someone from the surveillance team. Hattie was, therefore, protected by her own armed thugs, some of whom had quickly driven up from a bawdyhouse in San Antonio known as the Pony and Poodle Farm. Five sheriff's deputies and two rangers arrived, and before any shots were fired, the standoff was defused. Everyone not associated with law enforcement was disarmed. A few arrests were made for vagrancy and firearms investigation but nothing serious.

There was a six-day news blackout on the coup attempt at M&M Courts. Reporter Jim Berry purported to have ferreted out the story from facts that were "buried deep" in county files. Unfortunately, Berry's account is riddled with inaccuracies, rumor and propaganda planted by law enforcement. Ten years later, writer/filmmaker Robert A. Burns attempted to offer a fresh, irreverent take on the incident with a story in his pioneering alternative weekly *Free & Easy*, but his version isn't very reliable, either.[126]

The *Statesman* account is intriguing for the way it avoids admitting to the paper's collaboration in perpetuating a convenient civic myth. As recently as October 1964, the newspaper had described Hattie Valdes as "an almost forgotten Austin woman" who had "retreated into quiet retirement in 1960," claiming that, after four decades in the business, "she shuttered the last of 'Hattie's' places four years ago."[127]

The myth was helpful to Hattie and her facilitators, the most important of which was Travis County's chief law enforcement officer, Sheriff T.O. Lang. The ruse began in January 1953, when Lang began his first term in office with a well-publicized raid of Hattie's house at 5906 South Congress Avenue, along with two other brothels, one operated by Peggy Stephenson and the other by a woman named Delores. The headline that time was "Lang Closes 'Call Houses,' Says They Will Stay Closed," wink, wink. The houses would reopen a week or two later. Raids were well timed, usually with advance notice.[128]

When Hattie was jailed in 1955 at age fifty-two, she told a reporter that it was the first time she'd been prosecuted for running a bawdyhouse in her twenty years in Austin. The *Statesman* dutifully carried her announcement that she was quitting the business because "I'm getting too old for this sort of thing." For the next decade, despite highly visible evidence to the contrary, the press continued to pretend that the old madam was living in "quiet retirement."[129]

Her house at 5906 South Congress was padlocked by the sheriff under an injunction order in 1960 and burned down the following year.[130] Austin reporters who obviously knew better wove those facts into the official story, blind to the pink Cadillac and beehive of activity at her other operation at M&M Courts, located farther south at 8714 South Congress. She also operated a house in Cuero.[131]

"Gangsterism" not only fails to admit to past obfuscations but also repeats another whopper, saying that the much-celebrated madam had a policy of not employing local girls, which was given as the reason for her embargo on Tim and Jerry Ray's prostitutes. How could this be believed? Did all the girls commute? *Time* magazine refuted this in 1964, advertising Judy Cathey, a South Austin native, as Hattie Valdes's "star attraction."[132]

In mid-July 1965, Hattie spent some time chilling out at a Best Western in San Antonio. A *Statesman* reporter asked if it was true that she was trying to avoid a summons to appear before the grand jury. "I'm not scared of anything," she replied. The same detectives who'd given the bawdyhouse owner a ride to San Antonio for her protection had also planted the grand jury rumor in the press.[133]

"Gangsterism" was also the first of many major stories on the gang that did not identify Tim Overton, Jerry Ray James and other key gang members by name. Apparently, the local media had been informed that excessive publicity could be an issue in any upcoming criminal prosecutions in Travis County. The story about the M&M Courts fracas refers to Overton and James as "two men who rank first and third on the Austin police confidential list of the city's most notorious thugs." Number one, Overton, was described as twenty-four years old, a "convicted forger...arrested on charges of burglary, possession of narcotics and carrying prohibited weapons" with "three 1965 Cadillacs now registered in his name" despite the fact that he had "no visible means of an honest or legitimate means of support."[134]

Number three gave an unambiguous description of Jerry Ray James: he was number one's "closest companion...a heavyset ex–oil field salesman spawned out of East Texas in 1939...a specialized safe man." The gang was referred to as "a Texas-wide assortment of pimps, burglars, drug addicts and, as police files sometimes sum them up—men with records of everything on the book."

The article says that Overton and James had recently threatened Hattie, saying, "We're taking over this town anyway, so we will just take a percentage off the top of what you are taking in." Near the end of the article (and in a more detailed account published on July 17, 1965), we also learn that Overton had already shared his long-range plans with Sheriff Lang.[135]

Continuing, the story says that "a convicted forger" (Tim Overton) had made a "brazen approach" in the sheriff's office on Friday, July 9. "He came in here with a lot of allusions [*sic*] about what was going on," Lang said. "He wanted to know 'what kind of deal' I'd make. I didn't want any part of it and that's when I reached in the desk drawer and took out the pistol."

Sheriff Lang claimed that he chased the brazen thug out of his office at the point of his pistol. Why the chief law enforcement officer of the county did not arrest the ambitious pimp on charges of attempting to bribe a law enforcement official was not explained. It's also interesting that no other witnesses to the incident have ever come forward.

"[Sheriff Lang] got greedy," said Charles Schotz, offering a different take on the affair. "He wanted a much bigger cut of all the prostitution, and Tim went down there to straighten him out. Guns were drawn and all that, and then, the big confrontation happened at Hattie's. A week later, the story finally breaks and T.O. tells his bullshit version of events."

At long last, the paper got it right: M&M Courts was permanently closed, and Hattie Valdes had actually retired. For many years afterward, however, the capital city's most famous madam could be found holding court at various watering holes, including the Alamo Hotel and the Iron Gate Inn. Extrapolating from the criminal investigation files I've seen, she remained in contact with fringe characters like John Flanagan through the 1970s, by which time Flanagan was regularly flying large loads of marijuana and cocaine across the border in stolen airplanes.[136]

ON MONDAY MORNING, THREE DAYS after the M&M Court coup attempt and Tim Overton's bugging suit, a scandal over an illegal eavesdropping system at the county courthouse. The entire courthouse was bugged, with a control console in the basement and microphones in the jail and spaces where attorneys met with prisoners under the assumption of confidentiality.

"Attorney Blames Sheriff: Courthouse 'Bugged'" broke the story about the system, including the $10,000 control center in the basement, which had been installed between 1962 and 1964. Austin attorney Tom Higgins confronted a hearing of members of the Travis County Commissioners Court with a long list of allegations.[137]

The commissioners who were present (several were conspicuously absent) swore they knew nothing about the courthouse and jail being wired. An invoice had been filed for installation of "radio equipment" in November 1964. Sheriff Lang was asked to explain. Lang replied, not very credibly, that although the equipment existed, no one knew how to use it. Certainly it had not been used to record prisoners' privileged conversations with their lawyers. Lang did admit that two booths where prisoners saw visitors were bugged. "This is for the security of the jail," he said.

Higgins asserted that visiting booths designated for confidential consultations with attorneys were also bugged. Lang denied it.

Lang had also ordered equipment for recording conversations in homes, cars and offices outside the courthouse and jail. These devices, Higgins claimed, could be and were used in that manner with Lang's approval.

The sheriff got testy. "Prove it," he demanded, "if you got your proof."

Higgins had proof: tapes of recorded conversations in attorney-client conference rooms, in jail cells, on telephones and some conversations that had been made outside the jail. Higgins delivered the package to the FBI office in San Antonio, and an official FBI investigation was launched. The courthouse bugging scandal continued through the fall but eventually died

Shocker, 1965: first, Tim Overton's anti-surveillance suit and then the scandal that the Travis County Courthouse was completely wired with illegal listening devices. *Author's collection.*

The most beloved bug in Austin history, the old Terminix exterminator's icon, retired to Eddie Wilson's Threadgill's South. *Author's collection.*

down with an order to have the equipment removed. Full compliance did not come until sometime in the 1970s.[138]

"No citizen has any privacy," said Higgins, expressing a sentiment that sounds quite contemporary. "It doesn't matter who you are. You don't have to be a crook."

Lang walked away relatively unscathed. After serving twenty years in office, he was finally defeated for reelection by Raymond Frank in 1972. He retired to his South Austin home and, three years later, dropped dead of a heart attack while mowing his lawn.

As SUMMER GAVE WAY TO FALL in 1965, reporting on the Austin crime beat without using Tim Overton's name went from tricky to almost impossible. At least four follow-up stories on the progress of Overton's civil rights suit and police incidents appeared from September through December 1965.

There was more bad press at the end of September, as suggested by the headline "Gun-Toting Overton Holds Police at Bay Twice."[139] The same day depositions were being taken in the bugging suit, there were two tense, armed stand-offs between Overton and Austin police. After a patrol car followed Overton's Cadillac to the Westhill duplex, he and Judy Cathey, both armed with pistols, paced around the yard, cursing the patrol officers with impunity.

Austin police chief Robert A. Miles explained that his police force was currently confused about protocol under the new Code of Criminal Procedures. The officers didn't know if they had the right to set foot on Overton's property without an arrest warrant or not. And the twenty-four-year-old safecracker and pimp cynically exploited that fact, as he knew police business better than the average city patrol officer.

Throughout this period, Overton remained rooted in Austin. Bowen, Tisdale and Garrett were plying their trade in the casinos around Omaha, Nebraska, and Council Bluffs, Iowa. Jerry Ray James and Chester Schutz spent several weeks in Chicago. Their girlfriends did tricks to raise money for legal fees. Joan Taylor parked little Debi Dabbs with family members for the summer. She and James flew to Puerta Vallarta for a few weeks, with George O. Jackson doing the flying. Jackson became

The location of this shot is also unknown to me, but apparently it was a drugstore. Tuffy Korn said that he and Sonny Stanley probably hit every drugstore in Austin. *Courtesy of the NARA.*

longtime friends with director John Huston when he filmed *Night of the Iguana* in Puerta Vallarta. Jackson also met Elizabeth Taylor and Richard Burton during the filming, but he probably didn't realize, as the FBI later learned, that Fat Jerry was working on a scheme to rob Richard Burton's house in Mexico. Before James solved the logistics, however, other business called him and his paramour back to the States.[140]

Despite the gang's geographic separation, the burglaries, robberies and other gigs actually increased. Between November 4 and December 29, there were five bank burglaries in Kansas, each occurring in towns that fit the gang's modus operandi. It was during this period that some astute police investigator coined the term "traveling criminals."

Closer to Austin, Walter Bernard "Tuffy" Korn Jr. took his skills with a welding rig and a small crew from the East First B-Team thugs and hit the farm town of Coupland, burglarizing the State Bank and Thompson's Manufacturing Company.

A bucktoothed twenty-year-old, who was five feet, nine inches tall and 150 pounds, Korn was a pot-smoking, derby-wearing badass from the Chalmers Court projects with a killer pomaded ducktail, rolling low in a bucket of bolts on retreaded tires. Korn needed money for legal fees and child support, but also, he just loved playing cops and robbers. "We were doing shit all the time," Korn told me. "Our attitude was, 'We're gonna do what we're gonna do, just see if you can catch us.'"

When the *Dallas Times Herald* fired a shot over Austin's bow with an exposé about an Austin-headquartered crime wave, there were no pseudonymous references to Tuffy Korn, but his dedication to the outlaw lifestyle was central to its theme. The date was November 16, 1965, and the headline: "Austin Base for Thugs: Gangs Reported Working Varied Crimes in State."[141]

> *Austin has become home base for a band of traveling hoodlums who strike in cities all over the state on burglary, robbery and narcotics theft sprees,* The Times Herald *has learned.*
>
> *Sources said the capital city is the hottest spot in the state as far as traveling hoodlums are concerned.*
>
> *A dozen police characters are striking at supermarkets, banks and other businesses in Texas and other states from the Austin base.*
>
> *"They specialize in bank burglaries and operate both inside and out of Texas," one source said.*

As in the post-"Gangsterism" coverage in the *Statesman*, no individual names were used in the article, and it was packed with details on the gang's methodology and specific crimes. The Austin-based gang, it said, was responsible for bank burglaries and over $1 million in jewel burglaries in North Dallas.

"Strangely enough, one man seems to be the boss when they travel in Texas on a job," said an unidentified source, "and still another man takes over when they leave the state"—a statement apparently referencing the difference in leadership. In their Austin-based operations, Tim Overton was in charge; elsewhere, Jerry Ray James took over.

Prostitutes accompanied the gang on their travels; small businesses in various towns were used as fronts for money laundering and exchanging messages. Additional inside information and allegations were revealed in follow-up stories after Austin officials responded.

"What crime center here?" asked Chief R.A. Miles, speaking to an *Austin Statesman* reporter, in one of several flip denials of the Dallas report.[142] "Dallas doesn't need any help from us," Miles said. "They have enough of their own criminals. Dallas has long been known as a home for roving thieves."[143]

The Dallas-Austin feud continued through December and January. If they were planted stories, the feudists on either side of the fight played their parts well. Austin mayor Lester Palmer belatedly weighed in, telling the *Statesman* that he wanted a report from Miles about the allegations from Dallas in addition to certain incidents in Austin. Palmer came off sounding a little clueless.[144] "Palmer also said that he was never given what police department insiders believe is the hard-core truth about an attempted gangland takeover last summer of a then-flourishing prostitution house south of the city."

As he had done at other points in his life, under extreme duress, with complications closing in on all sides, Tim Overton went into hyper-drive. During the last weeks of 1965, in between bank burglaries and other heists, he led a series of upscale residential break-ins in which the scores were typically double or triple the amount they usually cleared on a small-town bank job. The jobs were immaculately timed strikes on houses and estates in the best of Austin addresses. In ten days (November 30 to December 9), five residences on the west side were looted of jewels, furs and other valuables.

In the last two weeks of 1965, there were two bank burglaries in Kansas and, in Austin, three more big residential scores. At the Harper residence in Tarrytown, the thieves took paintings valued at $8,500; from Chester Brooks, cash, jewels and coin collections worth $20,000; and from Hiram and Mabel Reed, jewelry, uncut stones and other valuables estimated at $60,000.

Some of the homeowners were wealthy gamblers, men known to have easily convertible valuables such as jewelry, gems and other collectibles. Hiram Reed, a member of one of Austin's oldest families and an independent oil operator, was emblematic. "Hiram loved whores, whiskey, and gambling," said George O. Jackson, whose then wife was Hiram Reed's niece.

Aside from profit, there was a revenge motive in at least some of the burglaries.

In recent weeks, a number of prominent citizens and civic leaders had begun holding meetings discussing ways to combat the crime problem in Austin.[145] On the heels of the publication of the *Dallas Times Herald* report labeling Austin a "crime center" (i.e., home of the Overton gang), two local groups formed, both with a primary purpose of paying for legal fees of the defendants in the federal civil rights suit filed by Tim Overton. One of the groups, the Travis County Grand Jury Association, was basically a defunct organization that was reactivated through the persistence of former grand jury foreman Hubert "Hub" Bechtol. Back in the 1940s, Bechtol was a three-time All-American at UT. He had a brief career in the National Football League with the Baltimore Colts.

In the '60s, as a real estate agent and civic leader, Bechtol tried, not always successfully, to promote his extreme agenda through the aegis of various establishment groups like the chamber of commerce and, in particular, the National Board of Realtors. In 1968, he vainly tried to torpedo Austin's fair housing ordinance in the hopes that rich, white fat cats like himself wouldn't have to live next door to people of color.[146]

The Greater Austin Association was a newly minted outfit. Besides petitioning local law enforcement and Mayor Lester Palmer to get tough on crime, the GAA also served as a fundraising group dedicated to paying legal fees for Harvey Gann and K.R. Herbert.

On the evening of December 20, 1965, Hiram and Mabel Reed left their home at 2623 Wooldridge Drive to go out for a light dinner. They were away from home less than an hour, ample time for Timmy and his crew to punch the wall safe and load up all the furs and other baubles, $60,000 worth.

Hiram, who had recently signed up with Bechtol's law-and-order posse, must have wondered if that had been a good idea.

# 6
# HELL HOUNDS ON THEIR TRAIL: 1966

Once upon a time, everyone said that Jerry Wix LeMond was a brilliant lawyer. If you argued with him about legal issues, even the most obscure, arcane points of law, you were bound to lose. "Almost every time, Jerry would end up being right," said Ed Wendler. "There was something magical about him. He was a genius, but an evil genius."[147]

LeMond's expertise also extended to precious metals, rare coins and gems, items that some attorneys and bail bondsmen accepted as barter for services or bought outright for cash. LeMond also mixed with the well-heeled, exotic fringe of the Texas underworld, people like Amon Carter III, one of the wealthiest men in Fort Worth.[148]

"He and Flanagan were real, real tight," said George O. Jackson. "That's how he got involved with the Overtons, fencing jewelry, and stuff like that."

In December 1965, Jackson and LeMond flew to Guatemala City, where there was a coin collection LeMond intended to buy. "His friend had given Jerry $25,000 cash to buy the collection outright," said Jackson, "but he liked dickering with the guy, so he'd go see him and buy a few pieces every morning. This went on for about a month." Afternoons were spent buying silver dollars from the locals over gin and tonics at the Pan American Hotel. Every night there were toga parties at the Pensión Carmen, staffed with girls from a bordello called Pinkie's.

"Then we came back and the shit hit the fan," said Jackson. "You see, Hiram Reed was my wife's [Lolly] uncle. That was her mother's brother. Now, I didn't know much about that, and I didn't want to get involved in it,

The Wheeler County deputy shot out the tires on the '64 Cadillac getaway car, alerting the burglars, who scattered across the empty, frozen plains. *Public domain photo.*

because those people [the Reed family] were real good friends of mine, but I do know that it had something to do with Tim."

That "something" was the general assumption that Jackson's friend Tim Overton had masterminded the $60,000 burglary at Uncle Hiram's home. But if Jackson was having a rotten New Year with the in-laws, he was nowhere near as miserable as Jerry LeMond.

LeMond's part of the "something" was going with Overton to Los Angeles, Houston and San Antonio to fence the booty from the Reed and Brooks burglaries. "Jerry was supposed to have all these connections," said Jackson, but Overton was disappointed in the amounts paid by LeMond's connections.

"Jerry was really in the shit about that," said Jackson. "Tim wanted to kill him."

Around midnight on January 13, the argument between LeMond and Overton got put on temporary hold. The surveillance microphone in the apartment at 4209 Speedway Avenue picked up a knock at the door, followed by what sounded like a cap pistol and other frantic noises. A patrol car materialized in record time followed by an ambulance ride to Brackenridge ER—side benefits of the surveillance state circa 1966.[149]

Pete Johnson drove down from San Antonio after hearing the news on the radio. Two Austin police officers stood guard outside Overton's hospital room. "They wouldn't let me in," said Johnson. "Tim heard me out there arguing with the cops and he said, 'Hey, is that Cottontail?' and they let me in. I asked him, 'Why don't you get out of all this shit? He said, 'Pete, they won't let me out.' Just like that. 'They won't let me.' I said, 'Who? Who won't let you out?' He wouldn't tell me."

The shooter, a mentally disturbed twenty-two-year-old man named Robin Turner, had recently been discharged from Austin State Hospital. The explanation he offered to homicide investigators suggested that he had intended to kill Tim Overton as a sort of public service. The bullet, fired from a .22-caliber rifle, a little squirrel-hunting piece, had entered low on the rear shoulder, nicked the left lung and narrowly missed the spine. Overton

The apartments at 4209 Speedway, where Tim Overton was shot by a mentally unstable man on January 13, 1966. *Author's collection.*

The owners of the complex at 4209 Speedway are probably unaware of the irony of the continued surveillance of the premises in 2014. *Author's collection.*

made jokes about it. Unaccustomed to being the victim, he refused to give police any information about the crime. He walked to the ambulance under heavy guard but unaided, claiming that he'd accidentally shot himself in the back while cleaning his gun.

At Brackenridge, X-rays showed the bullet to be so close to the spine that removing it would put Austin's number one badass at risk of permanent paralysis. If there was a snappy comeback for that, it's been lost to history.

ONE WEEK LATER, OVERTON WAS welcomed home from the hospital with a federal warrant, and at the LeMond family home at 6303 Mountain Climb Drive, "an evil genius" lawyer was taken into custody on the same charges.

The charges were transporting stolen property—i.e., forty items of jewelry, valued in excess of $4,000—from Austin to Beverly Hills, California, with the knowledge that the same had been stolen, a violation of the federal interstate commerce act.[150] LeMond and Overton were released on bond and appeared for arraignment in federal court in San Antonio on January 26. Both pleaded not guilty.

On February 23, 1966, LeMond agreed to meet FBI special agent Morton P. Chiles Jr. at the Night Hawk diner on Congress Avenue. The Night Hawk was known for its lush, red leather booths, grilled steaks and Texas toast, but on this night, plea bargain was on the menu. It was only one of countless attempts by the government to exploit the ugly rift that had developed between LeMond and Overton.

After the preliminaries, Chiles informed LeMond that if he didn't cooperate and testify against Tim Overton and his gang, he and Overton would be tried as codefendants for conspiracy in the interstate jewelry case, which would come to trial in January 1968.[151] LeMond said no dice. In this excerpt from a two-page FBI memo, Chiles summarizes LeMond's response:[152]

> *He explained that on January 19, 1966, after he had been released on bond, Tim Overton came to his home with two of his associates and took him for a "ride." He was told by these men not to talk. He said because of this incident he had been placed in fear of his own safety and particularly the safety of his wife and his children. For this reason LeMond advised that he could not furnish any information. He further indicated that he would like to furnish the FBI all the facts involved in this matter but he felt that under the circumstances he could not do so.*

On the morning of January 20, 1966, LeMond had been admitted to Brackenridge, having suffered "multiple contusions, abrasions and bruises over the extremities of the body and two rib fractures." An alcoholic who had survived a prior bout with hepatitis, he was also advised to stop drinking immediately. But there were things that scared Jerry LeMond more than the federal government or death. He died of liver cancer on Valentine's Day 1970.[153]

He never talked.

THE YEAR 1966 WAS STILL IN diapers when the Austin crime beat gave up trying to avoid mentioning the name Overton in the news. On January 3, burglars struck Farmers State Bank in Bertram, a town fifty miles from Austin, scoring about $14,000 from the vault. As the FBI well knew, Overton was in Beverly Hills partying on liquidated Brooks and Reed booty. Bertram was the work of Tuffy Korn and his East First Street B-Team, who partied on Galveston Island for a few days after burying a portion of the loot in a chicken coop. A week later, they were all in Travis County jail, trying to hustle up bail.

On January 31, Chester Schutz, Ben Tisdale and Dale Hall broke into the First State Bank in Pond Creek, Oklahoma and sacked up the contents of the vault and twenty-one safety deposit boxes. Leaving the bank under shotgun fire from the police, Mary Farmer drove the getaway car. They slipped through the city dragnet and turnpike roadblocks, returning safely to their hideout at 4538 South Fern Street in Wichita, Kansas.

On February 26, 1966, Curtis and Wynan Newsom drove a '61 Chrysler Imperial to Austin to repossess a '62 T-Bird and a hooker named Marci. *Courtesy of the* Vernon Record.

On February 4, a swarm of police cars descended on Fern Street and arrested the whole party. The FBI was involved, as was the Kansas Bureau of Intelligence (KBI) and city police from Wichita and Oklahoma City. Ernie Scholl was on the Fern Street stakeout, taking surveillance photos for just under two weeks. After the arrests, Scholl meticulously examined Chester Schutz's burglary kit—tools that Scholl had surreptitiously marked during a drug raid at Schutz's home in Austin the previous August.[154]

Chisels and punches were vital tools for peeling and punching vaults, locks and safes, and they left unique microscopic "fingerprints" at the point of impact. The confiscated tools were found to match indentations left at several different bank burglaries. Scholl's expert testimony on such forensic evidence in the 1968 conspiracy trial would prove to be crucial in making the case for the prosecution.

The government's case against Tim Overton was still fraught with difficulty. The federal case against him in the interstate jewelry trial was instructive. When the case was tried in San Antonio in January 1968, none of the buyers that Overton and LeMond met with (in Beverly Hills, San Antonio and Houston) was willing to testify that Overton had uttered a word during the transactions for the loot. If they were to be believed, Overton just came along for the ride, and it was all LeMond's deal.

Overton retained Fred Semaan of San Antonio, one of the top criminal attorneys in the state. With no witnesses willing to state that his client did anything but hang out during the transactions, Semaan devised a simple strategy and refrain: "Mere presence is not proof of guilt." The jury voted to acquit.

JUST WHEN IT SEEMED THAT the Overtons would get through the month of February without another major headline, Darrell Overton shot a Dallas pimp named Curtis Eugene Newsom.

On Friday night, February 26, Newsom cruised into town behind the wheel of a white '61 Chrysler Imperial, the kind with tail fins like an albatross.[155] Sharing the front seat were Newsom's brother Wynan and his wife, Charlotte. They sloshed through the bars in East and South Austin searching for a short, skinny coffee shop waiter named Jimmy Taylor, and for Marci, a prostitute formerly in Newsom's employ who had defected from him for Taylor. Marci used the last name Newsom even though she was legally married to a man named Cadillac Perkins. The other prize sought by the Newsoms was a 1962 T-Bird that Marci had driven to Austin when she left. Curtis wanted it back, even though the car wasn't in his name and she was the one making payments on it.

On March 13, 1966, the gang was busy in Graford; they hit one bank and two grocery stores. *Courtesy of the NARA.*

Meanwhile, little Jimmy Taylor was way up north at 5325 Burnet Road, working the night shift at the Toddle House. His South Austin landlord William O. McClusky phoned to say that the Dallas threesome had come by Taylor's garage apartment looking for the him, the T-Bird and Marci. The men were big, drunk, armed and mean.

"Jimmy," McClusky told him, "those people are not here to give you a Valentine."

Taylor called Darrell Overton, and they met up at his apartment at 2304 South First Street. Overton's girlfriend, Mildred Ross, waited outside in his Volkswagen bus.

The trio returned about 4:30 a.m. Wynan, a Korean army veteran, retreated after being shot in the arm. Newsom went inside and got a kneecap blown out by a slug from Overton's .38. Taylor had a twelve-gauge shotgun loaded with double-aught buckshot. As Newsom lay crippled on the floor, Jimmy Taylor stuck the muzzle of the shotgun in the pimp's face and pulled the trigger. According to descriptions in the legal case files, the blast all but severed Newsom's head from his body.[156]

ON FRIDAY, MARCH 4, THE A-Team—Tim Overton, Jerry Ray James, Hank Bowen and an ex-con from Chickasha, Oklahoma, named William Robert "Lucky" Brown—hit a bank in Strawn, Texas, population eight hundred, in Palo Pinto County, 260 miles north of Austin. Over the weekend, Overton drove back to Austin and bought for $1,125 a '61 Cadillac with low mileage, formerly owned by a doctor. He put the title in the name of Star Steel Erection Company, Texas registration number BFB 711. On Saturday night, Tim Overton joined his father and stepmother at Ernie's Chicken Shack for dinner and the Jets' soulful renditions of the weekly top ten songs.[157]

Meanwhile, Bowen and James robbed a pharmacy called Krank's Drug Store in Wichita, Kansas, and then drove to Midland. There Bowen traded in his '66 Buick for a bronze '64 Cadillac DeVille sedan.[158]

The party moved on to Amarillo, the ranching and energy industry hub of the Panhandle famously mentioned in "Route 66," the great song about old U.S. 66, America's fabled "Mother Road." Two rooms were booked at the Holiday Inn using fake names. Lucky Brown checked in at the Palo Duro Motel. James rented a new drill at Sears on March 11.

On Sunday, March 13, the quartet slinked into Graford, another dinky town in Palo Pinto County. It was a busy night; they knocked over one bank and two grocery stores.

The First State Bank of Mobeetie in 2010, looking toward the dump road where the '64 Cadillac was parked on March 14, 1966. *Author's collection.*

One of the roads leading out of Mobeetie. Out there is a whole lot of nowhere to run. *Author's collection.*

After midnight on March 16 in Mobeetie, population two hundred, they broke into the First State Bank, but they were just getting started on the vault door when they heard gunfire outside. A half mile away, the road to the town dump cut across a snow-and-ice-crusted field. A deputy from Wheeler County had sped to town after being alerted by the night watchman, who had called the county dispatcher from inside the beauty shop after watching the thieves pull up at the bank in the Cadillac. Now the deputy was shooting out the tires. He missed a few times, so there were quite a few shots.

The thieves erupted from the bank's back door and scattered across the dark, empty plains, writing a new chapter in the outlaw history of the Texas Panhandle. I traveled to the scrawny little town of Mobeetie in 2010. From its forlorn, ragged appearance, I was not surprised to find that the population number had not budged since 1966. The land seems so plain and empty it takes your breath away and almost feels like an insult. Then the horizon fills up 180 degrees all around with the dark fury of a thunderstorm.

Standing in the middle of the road next to First State Bank of Mobeetie, with no fear of being hit by a passing vehicle, looking out at the knife-edge horizon, I kept thinking: out there is a whole lot of nowhere to run.

The Panhandle comprises over twenty-five thousand square miles, nearly 10 percent of the state's total land area. Despite its sparse population, the area has a wild and violent history, having been the crossroads of Spanish conquistadors, Plains Indians, bison hunters, cattle drives, oil boomtowns and infamous western lawmen and outlaws. This is where the gang met its Waterloo.

POLICE HAD BEEN ON ALERT for over a week in New Mexico, Oklahoma, Kansas and Arkansas. Within an hour of the deputy's rash gun shots, a hurricane of activity descended on Mobeetie, Wheeler County and hundreds of miles all around. By dawn, a massive manhunt was underway. There were mounted deputies and rangers and volunteers on foot, in airplanes and in helicopters. Bloodhounds and deer-tracking dogs came in from as far away as Magnum, Oklahoma.

Less than twenty-four hours earlier, Ernie Scholl himself had been working the area. He had left Amarillo on Tuesday morning, spending the next ten hours driving back to Austin, where he had a home in the Brentwood subdivision, just off Burnet Road. He ate dinner with Jeanette, the wife who rarely saw him anymore. Abour 5:00 a.m., he got one of those calls a detective expects in the middle of the night, but this one was good news. "We got 'em," said the voice of Doyle Ramsey, a Wheeler County deputy.

Scholl woke up Harvey Gann, called the director, requisitioned a pilot and airplane and touched down on a little strip in Wheeler just after sunrise. Before going into the jail, he muddied his boots and pant legs. He wanted the fugitives to think he'd never left. "One of those mind games," he called it.

James and Bowen had been in custody since just before dawn, pulled out of a stolen pickup truck with a .30-caliber carbine and $3,400 in cash. Twelve hours later, Freddie Hedges was arrested near the oil ghost town of Magic City. He'd made it ten miles south of Mobeetie, a run even more impressive than in the fall of '56, when, with Midland down 12–0 against the Arlington Heights Yellowjackets, Freddie fired up the Bulldogs' comeback by scoring on an eighty-nine-yard kickoff return.

Newspapers all over the state carried the news: "Bloodhounds Searching for Bank Burglars," "3 Held, 2 Hunted in Bank Burglary," "Bank Robbery Attempt Fails," "Austin Man Captured as Bank Burglary Suspect, Four of Five Now in Custody" and, on Friday, the third day after the break-in, "Tim Overton Held in Bank Burglary."[159]

Sadly, the press was unaware of all the ways that the manhunt had been bungled, including how the hapless Amarillo Police Department's stakeout turned slapstick at the Holiday Inn. (Space limitations also preclude a fuller account here.)

By Friday morning, Overton and Lucky Brown had covered thirty miles on foot. At Lela, they stole a dump truck and sped west on Route 66, heading for Amarillo, maybe all the way to New Mexico. Sixty miles later, near the Panhandle, they crashed through a roadblock, veered off the highway and crashed into a butane tank. In a Hollywood film, the tank would have blown sky high, and the villains would have escaped. But the tank did not blow up. The wrecked dump truck was abandoned, and the burglars, now on foot, split up. About 1:30 p.m., bloodhounds tracked Overton to a vacant house. Cold, dirty and unarmed, he surrendered peacefully.

Brown continued on foot to Pantex, a company town that produced nuclear and chemical weapons. If this was a movie or a video game, the cops would've closed in, with lots of shooting and chasing through a hellish rat's maze of pipes and machinery up to the very top of the most explosive thing in the complex. In a fever dream final exchange of taunts with police on fuzzy megaphones, Lucky Brown would fire his gun, igniting a nuclear holocaust, and just as the mushroom cloud enveloped him, he would shout maniacally, "Good-by, suckers! Top of the world, ma!" But this was not a movie or a video game.

Brown knocked at a door and a nice man answered. A security guard at the plant, he gave Brown a ride to Amarillo, a distance of thirty miles. After dropping him off, the security guard thought about Brown's story about getting drunk and his car breaking down and then falling in the ditch and getting all muddy. The guard had heard about the bank burglars. He decided to call the police.

If Brown had simply picked up his car and left Amarillo, he might have earned his nickname. But he stopped at the Holiday Inn and got his car, a red '65 Impala, and drove it to the Palo Duro Motel, where he took a shower, then went to Denny's and ordered breakfast. Before he had time to finish, he was interrupted by lawmen wanting to know if he was the owner of the Impala in the parking lot and would he mind showing them his registration papers? He was escorted outside, and when he opened the glove compartment, the sun glinted off a pistol inside, and the jig was up for William Brown.[160]

By Friday evening, five alleged bank burglars had been arraigned before the Wheeler County justice of the peace. A vast amount of evidence was seized from the bank, four motel rooms, four vehicles and the suspects' clothing. There were safecracking tools, locksmith equipment, gaming paraphernalia, weapons, ammunition, hoods, ski masks and gas masks. Reading material included *In Cold Blood* by Truman Capote, an Aldous Huxley novel, rare coin price guides and the 1965 edition of *Southwest Bank Directory*. They had enough pills to medicate an army, thirty cartons of cigarettes, pilfered chewing gum, condoms, aspirin, sunglasses and more than enough quality menswear to open a clothing store.

After arraignment on federal charges in Amarillo, Jerry Ray James was transferred to Gulfport, Mississippi, where he would be tried for armed robbery of the Red Carpet Club. After a good deal of wrangling, bonds were set and eventually secured for the other four.

BACK IN AUSTIN FOR LESS than a week, Tim Overton pulled up at 3502 Goodwin Avenue on the morning of April 11 to find an inquest in progress. His father had overdosed on pills and whiskey during the night. A cameraman for KHFI-TV followed him inside. Overton warned Travis County justice of the peace Jerry Dellana against allowing cameras in the house. Dissatisfied with Dellana's reponse, he punched the cameraman, called the police a bunch of dogs and, according to Dellana, threatened his life. Overton was subdued and taken into custody.

Florine Craine, no big fan of Overton, blamed it all on the police. They had talked her into calling him and promised to keep cool, but as soon as he walked in, "the Austin police jumped on him…they had a big fight, at which time the Austin police drew their guns and created a great disturbance."

Finus Overton's death was ruled a suicide. Tim pleaded guilty to a charge of simple assault and paid a fine of $200.

Tim Overton's anti-bugging suit against APD came to trial; the jury found APD at fault, but the judge reduced the damages to one dollar. To Harvey Gann, it was a big joke. "I think one of my friends pitched in and paid the dollar for me," he said.

It was a year for strange crime. In January, James Cross Jr. was convicted and sentenced to life for killing two University of Texas co-eds, Susan Rigsby and Shirley Stark. Rigsby and Stark, both Chi Omega sisters, had disappeared on Sunday, July 18, 1965, the same weekend Austinites belatedly learned of the attempted takeover at M&M Courts. Stark's yellow Corvair was found on the north side of town. A frantic search made headlines. The police searched the area near the car but somehow missed the body. A psychic said some spooky things. On the twelfth day, on return to the weedy lot where the Corvair had been dumped, the wind changed, bringing the smell of death. The bodies were found fairly close to the location the psychic had predicted.[161]

Now, on July 16, 1966, almost exactly a year later, an even worse story gripped the nation: Richard B. Speck, a twenty-four-year-old former meat truck driver, ex-con and petty thief, had systematically tortured, raped and murdered eight student nurses in Chicago. Media coverage, using headlines like "8 Student Nurses Butchered in Dorm" freely mixed puerile fascination with disgust in reportage of the 150-minute "horror orgy."

A sunnier mood prevailed on Sunday, July 31, the first day of the Austin Aqua Festival, an earlier era's chamber of commerce version of South by Southwest (SXSW) and Austin City Limits festival but with powerboat races and water follies mixed in. The list of big celebrities started with cast members from the new *Batman* film, not the Dark Knight vision of the superhero but the campy, comic mid-'60s version. Comic actor Adam West as Batman

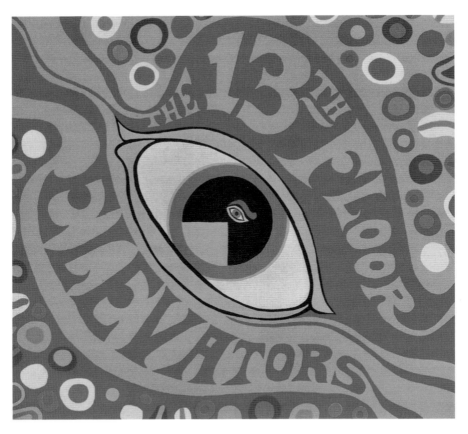

The first album by the 13th Floor Elevators, *The Psychedelic Sounds of the 13th Floor Elevators*, a band that was much disliked by the police.

fought cute, hapless villains in fights that were cartoonish and bloodless, the screen peppered with sound effect balloons like "POW!" "ZAP!" and "KA-BLOOM!" A carefully orchestrated Batmania mob scene at the airport was followed by a parade down Congress Avenue and a premiere at the Paramount Theater.

The euphoria faded the next day, Monday, August 1, the day of the Tower massacre at UT by Charles J. Whitman, who died in a hail of bullets and shotgun blasts, still owing Tim Overton that $200 poker bet. It would be fascinating to know what Overton said when he learned the identity of the Tower sniper.

ONE MORE PIECE OF '60S synchronicity is worth mentioning. Since the beginning of the year, and even going back to December, Austin's most notorious burglars and a popular rock band had been crossing paths with a regularity that seems almost eerie.

The 13th Floor Elevators are recognized today as the iconic band that invented psychedelic rock. The singer was the remarkable nineteen-year-old Roky Erickson of South Austin. Offstage, Erickson was sweet and soft spoken, but onstage, he was a force of nature. He had Mick Jagger/Little Richard charisma and grit and an uncanny ability for composing perfectly formed rockers and ballads.

Erickson's previous band, the Spades, started in early 1965, was a prototypical '60s garage rock outfit and a strong draw at clubs like the Jade Room and Le Lollypop. The last gig the Spades played was on December 2. The new band played its first gig on December 8. Erickson was the front man for drummer John "Ike" Walton, bassist Bennie Thurman and guitarist Stacy Sutherland, all from the Lingsmen, another fairly typical '60s rock band. The Elevators also featured an acid guru named Tommy Hall on electric jug. With their first gig at the Jade Room on December 8, 1965, the band attracted a fervent cult following and made music history.[162]

Not everyone following the band was a fan. As it was later revealed, the band was under constant police surveillance since its inception. In Austin, the effort was led by city detectives Harvey Gann and Burt Gerding, and their counterparts elsewhere in Texas hounded the Elevators everywhere they played. More than once, the band had to play gigs on borrowed equipment after the police, in a vain search for drugs, had dismantled theirs.

The Elevators' first single, "You're Gonna Miss Me," was a local hit until it was banned from KNOW, the local AM radio station. The ban was announced just prior to the band being busted for marijuana possession on January 27, 1966.[163]

Decades later, Gerding and Gann articulated the rationale for their vendetta against the band. In the Roky Erickson documentary *You're Gonna Miss Me* (2005), Gann reiterated his support for harsh penalties for young, first-time drug offenders. "I always felt like if they'd have sacrificed a few kids, giving them a five-year lick or two [it would] give them the idea, 'Hey, don't fool with it.'" In 2006, Gerding offered an almost identical explanation for using police-state tactics against Thorne Dreyer, publisher of the '60s underground paper *The Rag*. "You started the cultural revolution," he told Dreyer, "and I felt strongly about my culture."[164]

The Elevators continued to grow in popularity in Texas and nationally, and on March 16, the day that Austin's best-known thugs were being chased by bloodhounds across the frozen Panhandle, Erickson and the Elevators were playing a packed room at the popular New Orleans Club, the show being broadcast live on a hip Austin station, KAZZ-FM.

The band's day in court, originally slated for September 19, 1966, was moved up to August 8 of that year. Austin's psychedelic trailblazers should have anticipated a swift conviction and stiff sentences. But due to a combination of clever lawyering, judicial inexperience and police screw-ups, the case fell apart. Charges against two members were suspended, and charges against drummer Ike Walton and Roky Erickson were dropped.

Both the Spades and the 13th Floor Elevators played weekly residency gigs at Le Lollypop, one of the Overtons' favorite Austin joints. It seems inevitable that Overton and the boys would catch Erickson's act, probably a number of times. Perhaps they interacted. Overton could've slipped Erickson a joint or a handful of Benzedrine. Erickson might've turned them on to a few hits of LSD.

No one's been able to say if it happened or not, but it might explain some of the crazy things that happened around 1966.

# 7

# They Didn't Care: 1967

Even before the "Summer of Love" in 1967, you only had to drive down the Drag to see Austin's old, square corners melting into new, cooler shapes, and it wasn't just the long hair and beads or the protests. The Drag was where you went to pick up *The Rag*, the first underground newspaper published in the south. *The Rag* not only served as a voice for left-wing politics, but it also helped lay the foundation for a new, hip community in the capital city. Music was a big part of that, as were features like Gilbert Shelton's underground comic strip, *The Fabulous Furry Freak Brothers*.[165] Peace signs outnumbered American flags down there. To question authority was almost the default position.

But Austin was still part of Texas, and it wasn't all peace, love and understanding. There were still, for example, places like the Conoco gas station at Thirty-fourth and Guadalupe Streets, where black customers and longhairs were frequently verbally harassed and beaten.

The owner, Don Weedon, a highly vocal UT alumnus, had played tackle for Texas back in 1939.[166]

"Don Weedon was the quintessential redneck bully, our generation's nightmare," said Eddie Wilson. "Weedon carried a rubber hose in his pickup and bragged about running longhairs off the road. There were stories about both longhairs and blacks who had their windows smashed at the gas station. Some were pulled from their cars and slapped around. Others had gasoline pumped into the car window."

Nor was Austin in the '60s a place of enlightened police interrogation techniques, a fact that was impressed on Tuffy Korn on numerous occasions.

Roy Q. Minton told me about the time two lawmen drove Korn out to a creek just north of town and water boarded him.[167] The lawmen, Texas Ranger Bill Wilson and Sheriff Bobby Kinser of Hays County, tied Korn to a rope and repeatedly dunked him in the creek to get him to talk. "It was standard Texas Ranger stuff for those days," said Minton, who told me this particular story and swore it was "the damn truth."

The sheriff was "a good guy," Roy said, while the Texas Rangers "were just terrible" in those days. "But Bobby and Bill had Tuffy on that rope, and they would pull him up out of the creek and bring him around and say, 'Are you ready to talk?'"

Although I had recently spoken to Tuffy Korn so I knew he hadn't died during this crude version of water boarding, it was still a little excruciating to hear about.

"But one time they pulled him up and he didn't come around," said Minton. "They kept on slapping him and shaking him and he ultimately came around. But before he did, Bobby said to Bill, 'Goddamn, Bill, if he's dead we're going to be in a peck of trouble. What in hell are we going to do? What are we going do?' Bill said, 'I know what we're going to do with him. I haven't made up my mind what I'm going to do with you.'"

The lawyer's ornate, hand-tooled cowboy boots perched on the corner of his desk as he told the story. At the end he laughed, and I laughed, too.

"Bobby Kinser told me that story," he said. "Once I told it to a group of fifty or sixty law enforcement officers, and you'd think they would be sensitive about something like that, but they laughed until they were crying."

That day I asked Minton about several other former clients and received more insightful anecdotes. In exchange, I was often able to answer his inquiries.

He was glad to hear that Korn was still around.

"Tell Tuffy to come by and see me sometime," he said.

And then there was Harrison County, Mississippi, whose chief law enforcement officer was Sheriff Eddie McDonnell. A caricature of a fat, corrupt, redneck southern sheriff, McDonnell wore expensive tailored suits in gaudy colors and bragged about the size of his bribes and his diamonds.

*Opposite, top*: The back door was drilled at the First State Bank at Kosse, Texas, and the vault opened with a cutting torch. *Courtesy of the NARA.*

*Opposite, bottom*: The vault at Kosse was opened with a cutting torch (see tanks at back left). Papers inside the vault caught fire, adding to the bank's loss. *Courtesy of the NARA.*

Besides protecting the casinos in his county, he befriended the worst crooks, pimps and killers in his domain.[168]

The only surprise about Fat Jerry James's "escape" from Harrison County jail in Gulfport, Mississippi, was that the sheriff hadn't given him a county vehicle and a full tank of gas. James had turned up missing on December 28, 1966, one day before federal marshals were to take custody. During his eight months of incarceration in Harrison County, James had been given a wide array of privileges and responsibilities. After James was convicted for the armed robbery of the Red Carpet Casino in Biloxi, Sheriff McDonnell made him a trustee at the jail. In addition to his official duties, James was given the use of a county vehicle to commit burglaries.[169]

When James went before district judge Dan Russell in November to plea for bail while his case was waiting to be heard by the Mississippi State Supreme Court, the sheriff appeared as a character witness, vouching for James that "he would be a good risk for bail…has been given many liberties, including running errands in town, traveling alone, and going to the barbershop." The request was denied.

Joan Taylor had moved to Gulfport to be with her man. She got an apartment and did tricks, dated a NASA engineer who wanted to marry her, worked with a pimp named Dick Head and danced in a strip club. Sheriff McDonnell checked in on her regularly in case she needed anything.[170]

On December 29, 1966, federal marshals were scheduled to take custody of James, but apparently someone called ahead of time. The day before the marshals came, James disappeared. For the next thirteen months, he lived the life of a desperado. It was a wild, nomadic life punctuated with periods of semi-domesticity, caring for their little dogs, going to the races and visiting with James. They lived for several months at a time in Gretna, Louisiana; Tulsa, Oklahoma; Tucson and Phoenix, Arizona; and then Tucson again. The feds finally caught up with the couple in Tucson in late January 1968 where, as Mr. and Mrs. Jerome Jennings, they shared a house on the edge of the desert with another outlaw couple, Wayne and Kam Padgett of Tulsa, Oklahoma.

During those thirteen months as a federal fugitive, Jerry Ray James committed countless burglaries and robberies, including brutal home invasions. Car dealers in Oklahoma were particularly helpful in trading one late model muscle car for another. James never lacked for friends and enablers.

*Opposite, top*: The morning after the investigation in Evant. Welding gear and other tools were left behind. *Courtesy of the NARA.*

*Opposite, bottom*: Evant, Texas. *Courtesy of the NARA.*

James started wearing a cowboy hat and boots and spent lots of time with horses. Sadly, it wasn't until his eighth month on the lam that he achieved his oft-stated ambition of making the FBI's most wanted list. The accession was announced in the *Brownsville Herald*, printed just down the coast from Corpus Christi, the town of his birth, with a catty shrug: "Corpus Christi Slick Makes it to Top Ten."[171]

In July 1966, when Overton's calendar was dotted with dates in federal court, he and his brother Darrell went shopping for walkie-talkies and another acetylene rig. They were not the quitting type.

The Mobeetie bust not only put an end to the gang's small-town bank burglaries but also yielded volumes of intelligence about the logistics, tactics and habits of traveling criminals. For example, on the morning of March 16, 1966, only hours after Hank and Fat Jerry were captured, Webbie Flanagan flew in to arrange for their bonds and release. Then he sped over to the Holiday Inn, where he was arrested after packing up all their belongings—not just suitcases but also weapons, burglary tools, gambling paraphernalia and stolen merchandise. These were truly the actions of a full-service criminal defense attorney—a thrilling film noir scenario.

Flanagan was determined to take possession of the four automobiles and all the valuables, weapons, gambling gear and even the fake gems. Although his right to seize the vehicles was challenged in court, he successfully asserted legal claim, a task made comically complex because the chain of title ownership was murky by design. Sometimes the cars they drove were registered to Star Steel Erection Company, a sham corporation, or Overton Motors or in the name of one of their friendly, junkie car dealer friends.

Flanagan had long attracted special attention from law enforcement. He was suspected of setting up heists, making introductions, fencing stolen goods and innumerable other nefarious deeds. That such a relationship was a trademark of what came to be known as the Dixie Mafia was already well known to the FBI as well as regional law enforcement. Outside Texas, two of the most important agencies involved were the Kansas Bureau of Investigation (KBI) and the Mississippi State Highway Safety Patrol (MSHP).[172]

Someone, possibly Rex Armistead of the MSHP, began using the term "Dixie Mafia" during the late 1960s heyday of the Overton/James group and their counterparts who were operating on the Mississippi Gulf Coast. In contrast to the Italian mafia, this organized crime network appeared to have no godfathers or established system of leadership.[173]

As with Fat Jerry James and Tim Overton, it was often a case of two or more thugs who would reach out to some other thugs whenever they planned to pull a heist. If there was a job in Iowa where a special kind of person was needed—safecracker, strong arm, bail bondsman, lawyer or crooked deputy—they would call other members of the group for recommendations. The Dixie Mafia was like a guild, a network of villains, an analog Craigslist of crime.

SEEN FROM AN AIRPLANE WINDOW, the outline of Lake Travis resembles a dragon, with the bulbous, southeastern portion being the head. Harvey Gann lived on one of the spikes of its lower back. When I pulled up in the drive, he came out, smiling like an old uncle. He wore a baseball cap, a short-sleeved shirt, shorts, dark socks and loafers. The house was a split-level, the bottom part hugging a slope down to the rocky inlet below, the dragon's spine.

After talking for an hour or so, we took a break. He seemed anxious to show me his houseboat, which was docked just below the house on a rocky inlet, the dragon spike. Inside the little cabin, he bent down to open a hatch. The water's surface was soon roiling with big, hungry catfish.

Harvey tossed food pellets at them.

"That's really cool," I said. "Those are big catfish."

"You like catfish?" he asked.

"Sure I do."

Harvey motioned at a long-handled gigging hook on the wall. "Want to gig a couple? Take some home for dinner?"

I had already accepted a beer. On another trip, Ernie Scholl joined us for a lunch of grilled steaks and baked potatoes. I declined. It didn't feel right.[174]

ERNIE SCHOLL TOLD ME THAT Captain John "Tuffy" Krumnow, who worked out of Waco and McClellan County, was one of the few Texas Rangers respected by the task force in Austin. Since so many banks hit by the Overtons were within two hours' drive of Waco, that was a good thing.[175]

Ernie's esteem for Tuffy Krumnow was not shared by Tuffy Korn.

"He arrested me up in a little town in McClellan County," Korn told me. "He cuffed me and took me to this jail that wasn't open yet, nobody was there. It was a cold, cold morning. So he put me against the wall outside there and parked his car so that the front grille had me pinned against the building. He said, 'Look here, boy, I'm the only Tuffy in this county. You best remember that, boy.' I said, 'Shit, I don't want to be in your county.'"

Rangers J.T. Seaholm and Jim Riddle flanking Tim Overton. Seaholm played football at UT (1951, 1956–67) and for the Chicago Bears in between (1954). *Courtesy of the* Austin American-Statesman.

EVEN AFTER HE BECAME A girlfriend-beating pimp, Overton never lost his sense of being a good old boy. Look at the picture of him on the steps of the federal courthouse in Austin flanked by a pair of Texas Rangers. He looks damn good, shoulders like an Iberian bull, with an open shirt collar beneath a dark suit and wearing expensive shoes. He's laughing, head cocked to his right, answering some wisecracking reporter with a joke of his own. The rangers are laughing. Everybody's having a great time.[176]

"Tim didn't care and Jerry didn't care," Betty King said, trying to explain how crazy they were.[177] "I remember one time we were living in Dallas and they showed up at our apartment. They were giggling and laughing and they said, 'Come out here.' They had a big old Cadillac. They opened the trunk and it was full of men's socks. Hundreds and hundreds of socks. They told Curt, 'You want some socks?' I don't know who would want so many socks. It was like they'd stolen them out of a train car or something, there were so many of them. Curt took all the socks he wanted and they giggled and laughed and hee-hawed all night long. I'm sure they were just loaded to the gills."

The photo of Overton and the laughing rangers was taken on Monday, May 15, 1967. It's not a stretch to say that he's imagining himself as a reincarnation of Al Capone. A few weeks before the photo was taken, a plea bargain in federal court in Amarillo had resolved the Mobeetie case. The components of the deal were: a plea of guilty, a four-year sentence and a promise by the United States attorney that no conspiracy charges would be filed for the bank burglary. Freddie Hedges and Hank Bowen also pleaded guilty.[178]

In an attempt to solicit empathy from federal judge Emmett Choate, who presided over the sentencing, attorney Vern Knickerbocker claimed that his client, Freddie Hedges, had been on his way to becoming an All-American halfback at UT at one time. H.J. "Doc" Blanchard, speaking on behalf of Tim Overton, hit the same notes, stating that his client had lettered as a guard at UT. The judge's retort: "They would have done better to stick with football."

An interesting historical note: the federal judge presiding during some court dates on the Mobeetie charges was Sarah T. Hughes, who had administered the presidential oath to LBJ on Air Force One on November 22, 1963.[179]

In other business in Austin on May 15, 1966, the day the photo was taken, Tim's elder brother Charles was being tried for burglarizing the First State Bank of Jarrell. It was a knucklehead job, five hours' hard work for $575 in nickels and dimes, exchanged at a grocery store for eighty cents on the dollar, amounting to roughly $100 each in a four-way split. A week or so later, Richard Hinton, one of the four burglars, ratted out the other three.

Rounding out this team were Travis Roy Erwin and Louis Dell Branton. Erwin, twenty-eight, buck-toothed and fat, drove a green Ford Edsel, plate number BBS 492, and was considered a proficient gambler by Las Vegans with deep pockets. (In 1979, Nevada-based gamblers funded Erwin's pinochle and gin rummy games with cellmate Jimmy Chagra, bilking the unsuspecting drug kingpin of tens of thousands of dollars.)[180] Branton, age thirty-three, was one of ten guys whose North Austin chop shop had been shut down by an FBI raid in April.

Everybody who wasn't in jail already was headed there soon. Charles Overton was in prison on a life sentence as a habitual criminal. Tim's other junkie brother, Darrell, was in Huntsville after a multiplicity of recent convictions. His final arrest came during a safecracking at North Loop Pharmacy the night before trial for the pimp murder.

So why was he at the federal courthouse on May 15, 1967, and why was he laughing?

On this day, Tim Overton was called to appear in court on a charge of obstructing justice. The government complaint was based on statements by

Betty Hinton, wife of Richard Hinton, in which she alleged that Overton came by the Hinton residence in South Austin and had told her to tell Richard that if he testified against Charles in the Jarrell trial, "he would not be able to walk the street or live in the city of Austin."

The guilty verdict, which came as no surprise, carried a five-year term. Overton already owed four years for Mobeetie. The interstate jewel trial was set for January and the big conspiracy trial after that. And yet there he was, stepping out to smile at the reporters' camera flashes and the glare of the sun, which he wouldn't be seeing much of for a few years.

"Tim didn't care," Betty said. "Jerry didn't care."

Why should they? They were the stars of their own private gangster movies.

# THE BIG CIRCUS: 1968

Through the spring and early summer of 1968, revelations about the Gulf of Tonkin and the North Vietnamese overrunning Saigon were proving that America had stumbled into a tragic foreign policy blunder. An assassin in Memphis felled Martin Luther King Jr. Riots and fire consumed United States cities in righteous outrage. Senator Robert F. Kennedy, the last great hope to forestall a Nixon presidency, was shot to death in the Ambassador Hotel in Los Angeles. In retrospect, the excesses and oddities of the Overton/James conspiracy trial seem of a piece with the druggy absurdity of the late '60s.

*Left to right*: Jerry Ray James, Freddie Hedges, Hank Bowen, William Brown and Tim Overton in custody in 1966. *Courtesy of the NARA.*

THE TRIAL WENT OUT ON the road like a rock festival or old-school circus. The indictment accused Tim Overton, Jerry Ray James and a total of twenty other individuals of running an interstate prostitution and bank burglary ring. Returned by the grand jury in the last week of 1967, the indictment named fourteen men and six women set to be tried in the little border town of Del Rio. Arraignments resumed shortly after the FBI arrests of Joan Taylor (January 24, 1968) and James (January 25, 1968).

But the big show began collapsing under its own weight less than halfway through the opening act. On April 1, the venue was moved (for various reasons) upriver to El Paso. The biggest and most expensive trial in the history of both cities, it finally ground to a halt on June 26, 1968.[181]

Almost fifty years later, the thing people really remember about it had nothing at all to do with the main event. I heard the story from Vern Knickerbocker first and a hundred times after that. Knick, as most people called him, was the defense attorney for three of the accused conspirators—Freddie Hedges, Ben Tisdale and Elizabeth Sherman. Knick's clients were all free on bond, but eight others, including Overton and James, were held over for the duration of the trial, and during those long months, they regaled their lawyers with enough tales about their escapades in crime and vice to write pulp fiction versions of the *Illiad* and *Odyssey*. Knick did offer a caveat, saying, "I don't know if they were all true or not," but what he saw with his own eyes was good enough.

"Tim would screw Judy [Cathey] between the bars of his jail cell," he said, "and we jiggered for him." Knick laughed and banged his fist on his dining room table as he described the scene. "One of the lawyers would bring Judy down there together for a visit, and then he'd 'jigger' for them, as we used to say. We'd keep an eye out for the jailer while they did it."

Perhaps such things helped relieve the tedium for the legal eagles. The defense team numbered fifteen at the beginning, but even at a slimmed-down team of seven (as various defendants were dismissed from the indictment), it was a tough job. Most of them were court-appointed and had no money coming in during the trial.

"We got caught one time," Knick said, "but it was Chester [Schutz] and Mary who got caught, not Tim and Judy. Oh, yeah, man, I tell you, that trial was a kick!"

JERRY RAY JAMES'S BRIEF TENURE on the FBI's ten most wanted list must have made him seem a natural choice for first position on the indictment, as seen below. The placement helped perpetuate the erroneous impression that he was the leader of the outfit.[182]

*The Grand Jury Charges:*

*On or about March 13, 1964 and continuing until on or about April 30, 1966, within the Western Dist of Texas JERRY RAY JAMES, CHESTER ARTHUR SCHUTZ, CLIFFORD HENRY BOWEN, JAMES TIMOTHY OVERTON, DARRELL WAYNE OVERTON, BENJAMIN THOMAS TISDALE, WALTER BERNARD KORN, TRAVIS ROY ERWIN, HARBEN LEONARD STANLEY, DALE NORWOOD HALL, CURTIS GLENN GARRETT, WILLIAM ROBERT BROWN, MARY FARMER, ELIZABETH AGNES SHERMAN, JOAN DOBBS TAYLOR, SUE OVERTON, JUDITH ANN CATHEY, MILDRED ROSS, FRED CLINTON HEDGES, JERRY WIX LEMOND conspired together and with each other to commit offenses against the United States, and performed various overt acts in furtherance of the conspiracy, in violation of Title 18, US Code, Section 371.*

"James Gang" has a catchy ring to it, but the prosecution clearly believed that Tim Overton was the leader at least some of the time, that the conspiracy began in Austin, that the Overton transmission shop was an operational headquarters (and "crime school") and that the Overton residence on Goodwin Avenue was also an important meeting place. The subpoena for Ernie Scholl commanded him to bring to court "all records pertaining to the Overton Crowd"; Jerry Ray James was not mentioned.[183]

The entire indictment is a little surreal, with its dense listing of separate charges and often mundane sounding lists of "overt acts" presented as proof of the conspiracy, but federal law allows great leeway to the prosecution, including the use of circumstantial evidence.

Most of the men on trial were already serving prison terms for the Mobeetie bank job and other cases listed in the indictment. Jurors might have wondered why the government would waste the time and money trying them again. In his opening statement and closing argument, prosecutor Ernest Morgan labored to explain concepts such as the "substantive charge" of burglarizing a bank and the "instant charge" of conspiring to do it. From the opening statement to the bitter end, Morgan also stressed the government position that prostitutes had subsidized the gang between jobs and were thus just as guilty as the men who broke into the banks, peeled the vaults and drilled the safes.

Sometimes Morgan's oratory went into overdrive. In his closing statement, he said of the defendants that they were guilty of "the wildest orgy of crime, the likes of which I don't know if it has ever occurred before." His personal vision of the United States system of justice verged on the harsh and unforgiving side: "Ladies and gentlemen...the last thing in the world I would want anything whatever to do with would be to convict an innocent man or a woman, but I say to you...next to that the thing that I would hate to see worse would be for guilty people like these to go free."[184]

THE FIRST MAJOR WITNESS FOR the prosecution was Florine Craine, the much-married former stepmother of the Overton brothers, who had been a party to so much felonious activity that she earned a place on the government's separate list of "unindicted co-conspirators."

Morgan relied on Craine to help make the case for the existence of a conspiracy, if not an organized criminal gang. He frequently cited Craine's testimony that Overton and James had argued in her presence about which one of them was the "leader" of the gang. Actually, the subject of discussion on that occasion was an *Austin American-Statesman* article that referred to Overton as being "ranked first...on the Austin police confidential list of the city's most notorious thugs." James objected, testified Craine, and a heated discussion ensued.[185]

On cross examination, Fred Semaan, attorney for Tim Overton, asked the witness how many times she'd been married and divorced, and she got mixed up. She also admitted that she had a terrible memory for dates and that, during the past few years, she had been a user of barbiturates. More effective, perhaps, were her claims that Tim and Charles Overton had threatened and physically abused her. "That's how I got some of these teeth knocked out," she told the court, later stating that she had, "believe it or not, become real attached to the boys," even if on one occasion, she had been compelled to shoot Charles in the leg.[186]

OUT IN THE FLAT SCRUB LAND, 270 miles from Austin, Del Rio had a population of thirty thousand people and about six times that many goats and sheep. The county jail was small and insecure, though suitable for quickies, as Overton and Cathey proved daily. The courthouse was cramped and ill furnished. New tables had to be built to display more than five hundred evidentiary exhibits, not counting the four-foot-tall cannonball safe. Thirty marshals were brought in for security.

In the United States District Court system, Texas is divided into four divisions: Northern, Southern, Eastern and Western. The cities of Austin, San Antonio, Del Rio and El Paso are all located within the Western District. A number of the crimes in the indictment had occurred within the district as well, which figured into the choice of Del Rio as the original venue. Del Rio was free of the taint of pretrial publicity but only briefly. On February 19, as the handcuffed defendants were being led from the courthouse, several of them spit, kicked and shoved a television cameraman and a newspaper reporter.

Headlines were juicy: "Gang Members Menace Media," "Newsmen Cursed at Criminal Hearing" and the concisely stated "Prisoners Spit, Kick Reporters."[187] The defense filed a flurry of motions pleading for change of venue. Judge Suttle denied them all.

The FBI heard that thugs were converging on the border region in preparation for a mass jailbreak and escape to Mexico. A search of the jail turned up hacksaws and other contraband in the defendants' cells.[188] On March 18, Ernest Morgan filed a motion for change of venue. The motion was granted, and everyone packed their bags for El Paso.

"THESE BURGLARS AND CANNONBALL safes, we didn't know anything about that," said Heygood Gulley, an attorney from Eagle Pass who was appointed to represent Dale Hall. "They were professional, that was their life," said Gulley. "During the trial, Tisdale, who was out on bail, got caught inside a building over the weekend, doing a burglary."[189]

At another point, Dale Hall became angry at Gulley, jumped up, took a swing at him, missed and was wrestled to the floor by federal marshals.

"After that," Gulley explained, "they found out that when the girls brought them soda water during the morning break, they were also putting something in the soda water. So that's why after the break they were pretty rambunctious."

George Thurmond, whose father was a district judge in Del Rio, represented Jerry Ray James and Joan Taylor.[190] "They were fascinating and they were all different," he said. "Jerry Ray James was not dumb at all. I had the feeling that anything he wanted to do, he could be a success."

TIM OVERTON NEVER MADE IT to the FBI top ten, but he scored his own public relations victories. On February 15, in a federal courtroom in San Antonio, a jury returned a verdict of not guilty in the interstate jewelry case. Jerry LeMond had been severed from the case but remained a co-conspirator. As the Del Rio/El Paso trial commenced, LeMond's attorney, former Travis County district attorney Les Procter, requested a continuance, again citing illness as the reason.

District judge Darwin S. Suttle dismissed the charges against William Brown on the grounds that he had already been convicted of conspiracy in the Graford case and that the current case would expose him to double jeopardy. The four other defendants convicted in the Mobeetie case—Tim Overton, Jerry Ray James, Hank Bowen and Freddie Hedges—remained on the indictment. The defense filed motions citing the same doctrine used by Brown's attorney (the legal term being *res judicata*, as in "the matter has been decided"), but such motions were repeatedly denied.

Suttle also granted Jerry LeMond's request for continuance, recognizing the inevitable reality that the attorney would never appear in a courtroom next to Tim Overton, whether that court was in Del Rio, in Austin or on the moon.

A HERD OF CHARGING RHINOS could not have convinced Ernest Morgan otherwise, but Tuffy Korn should not have been on this indictment. The same was true of Sonny Stanley, Travis Erwin, Darrell Overton and Curt Garrett. While it was true that each had been involved in criminal escapades with Tim Overton and certain others in the group, the evidence against them was, in the most charitable interpretation, insufficient for conviction. Some of it was so laughably incorrect that it put the whole case in a bad light. Possibly this explains Judge Sutton's repeated admonishments to Overton to cease making those barking dog noises whenever Morgan was near.[191]

Walter Bernard "Tuffy" Korn Jr. was a professional burglar and safecracker in his own right. As committed an outlaw as any of the bunch, Korn hated authority and authority hated him back. On January 30, 1965, he was arrested for vagrancy while leaving an Austin lounge called Mi Gran Lounge. A joint was found in his pocket. He was tried and convicted on the drug charge, which at that time meant about ten years in Huntsville. The summary of the appellate court's ruling (Roy Q. Minton handled the appeal) reads like a 1950s film noir. The main issue was the legality of the vagrancy charge, which led to the arresting officer finding the joint. Under the Austin vagrancy statute, Tuffy Korn did fit the profile: He was able to work but told the arresting officer that he had no job and no plans to get one. The summary also states that the officer knew that Tim Overton and several other individuals with criminal records were inside the bar at the time Korn was inside. Four days earlier, the Overton gang had hit the First National Bank of Evant. The police "knew" that the Overtons had done the job, but they couldn't prove it.

Roy Q. Minton labored heroically for two years on Korn's appeal and his other legal entanglements. Korn was equally relentless in breaking into small-town banks and drugstores. "Me and Dickie Goldstein must have hit every drugstore in town," Korn told me. "Dickie went for the dope, I did it for the cash. We were having fun. Later on, it got more serious."

Some of the bank scores were substantial, but it was a fast life and not always a brilliant one. The loot from the Bertram bank, mostly in coins, weighed down the trunk of his Ford so much that on the ride back, Korn had to strain to see over the hood.

Korn lived in a little rural pocket of town on Tillery Street with a barn and patch of grazing land. Sometime after New Year's Eve, when Korn was in Galveston partying, his friend Chuck Bauser came by to feed the livestock. The chickens had scratched up the ground in the chicken coop where Korn had stashed the money bags from Bertram. Bauser started talking to the FBI.

Korn, Sonny Stanley and Travis Erwin were fantastically persistent burglars. Within two weeks of the Bertram bank job, they got arrested for it, made bail and were out on East Sixth Street in Austin with a tubular lock key and a bag, filling it with coins from parking meters. Busted again.

The conspiracy charges against Tuffy Korn were dropped around the end of February. Sonny Stanley and Travis Erwin were removed from the case later. Each was remanded to prison.


READING THE TRANSCRIPT OF THE trial and the motions, briefs, notes and other documents in the case file summoned comparisons to Kafka, Looney Tunes and the trial of the Chicago Seven (which occured one year later). The judge was testy, irritable and persnickety about decorum and protocol. Attorneys had to raise their hands before going to the restroom. The defense asked for a mistrial dozens of times. Semaan, who made dozens of objections a day, clearly got on Suttle's nerves.

"Freddie was tough," said Knick. "He would start off making objections to every little thing, no matter how insignificant. Again and again and again. Pounding the table. Finally, after two or three hours, he'd make a good one and the judge would sustain him and the jury would smile. I mean, God could be up there and Freddie would argue with him."

A page of transcript during a pretrial hearing in Del Rio helps illustrate how the large number of defendants affected the pace of things. John Flanagan was called to testify about the admissibility of items seized from James's car in Amarillo, and after direct examination by George Thurmond, Morgan cross-examined, asking about the items one by one. There was some inherent humor involved, since everyone knew that Flanagan had hurriedly cleaned out the motel room, unaware that the police had it staked out. Flanagan feigned ignorance, and Morgan became sarcastic. With every new item introduced, each defense attorney was impelled to object on behalf of his client or clients.[192]

> MORGAN: Well, look here, in this box there are some work gloves, do you see those?
> FLANAGAN: I see those.
> MORGAN: And were your clients so far as you know in the kind of work that they needed to wear work gloves, men's work gloves?
> MR. SEMAAN: I object to the question, it is inflammatory and prejudicial insofar as my four clients are concerned.
> THE COURT: Overruled.
> MR. SEMAAN: And for the further reason that they are not bound by anything that Mr. James may have had in his possession or in any car, or the motel room.
> THE COURT: Overruled.
> MR. THURMOND: I further object, Your Honor, it is not shown whose gloves these are in any manner.
> THE COURT: Overruled.
> MR. KNICKERBOCKER: I adopt the same objection, Your Honor.
> THE COURT: Overruled.
> MR. RHODES: We adopt the objection just made, Your Honor.
> THE COURT: All right, overruled.
> MORGAN: And then there are some highway maps, in here, do you see those.
> FLANAGAN: If you say so.
> MORGAN: Do you see them?
> FLANAGAN: I guess they are highway maps, I would have to look at them, there are three of them here.
> MORGAN: And there is a 50-state road atlas, in here, is there not (indicating)?
> FLANAGAN: Yes, sir.
> MORGAN: And there is another pair of gloves, is there not?
> FLANAGAN: Yes, sir.
> MORGAN: And there is another pair of gloves, is there not?
> FLANAGAN: Yes, sir.
> MORGAN: And your clients were not engaged in manual labor, were they?
> MR. KNICKERBOCKER: I object, that calls for a conclusion.
> THE COURT: If he knows he can answer.
> MR. SEMAAN: On behalf of my clients who weren't even there, I object.
> THE COURT: All right, overruled.

Objections to the gloves continue for another page and a half. Little wonder that the transcript runs almost nine thousand pages. Reading the transcript in the comfort of my office, I found myself becoming addicted to the minutiae, the strange, dry humor.

Later, Morgan introduced a bottle of pills. After the usual number of objections (all overruled), Morgan asked, "None of your clients is a practicing physician?...

One of many Kansas banks hit by the gang between 1964 and 1966. *Courtesy of the NARA.*

As far as you know they are not druggists or anything like that?" The next item was a key-cutting machine. Flanagan had no idea what it was, he said. He'd never seen one before. What about the little book, the one titled *Southwestern Bank Directory*, with the First State Bank of Mobeetie circled? Looks like a book about banks, Flanagan said. Didn't he know what these things were before he loaded them into the car trunk? He didn't, he said, he just gathered everything up and stuck it in the trunk.

Unlike criminal trials in movies, the most dramatic moments in the courtroom aren't always the ones that determine the course of the trial. One of the most devastating blows to the defense came during the first week of testimony, when Ernie Scholl took the stand to identify burglary tools that he had secretly marked during a drug raid at Chester Schutz's residence in Austin on August 30, 1965. The tools Scholl had marked also left telltale indentations at various bank jobs.

The defense team objected and argued against the admissibility of the burglary tools. One of the more interesting points raised during the arguments was Schutz's version of the drug raid, which was quite different from Ernie Scholl's. Schutz's account of the raid had been chronicled in the wording of a lawsuit filed in district court after his arrest. The suit accused the six arresting officers—Lieutenant Harvey Gann and Detective Tommy Olsen of the city vice squad and Ernie Scholl, E.J. Stutts and Darrell R. Moore, all of the State Narcotics Unit—of serious violations of his civil rights. According to the petition, filed by attorney Brooks Holman, the cops kicked in his door; then, as he entered, they jumped on him and "viciously attacked and beat him on the face, head, skull, chest, back, kidneys and legs." The complaint further alleged that Schutz was forced to state that the injuries had been incurred elsewhere and was told that if he told anyone otherwise, there'd be another beating. He also said the drugs were planted.[193]

Ernie Scholl, testifying under oath in Del Rio, claimed that there was no beating of the prisoner. School also assured me that the beating never happened, even though he was in the shed marking Schutz's tools when the alleged beating took place, so he would not have seen it personally. After all the challenges were filed, debated and considered by Judge Suttle, the tools were admitted.

The Mobeetie case reaped literally a truckload of evidence. There were numerous grounds for legal challenges. The most interesting challenge—and, in some ways, the most climactic debate of the trial—centered on the plea agreement in the Mobeetie case in federal court in Amarillo in April 1967. In that trial, United States attorney Pat Mulloy agreed that, in exchange for the defendants' guilty pleas, no conspiracy charges would be filed.[194]

Now, during the third week of May 1968, attorney Fred Semaan argued on behalf of a defense motion that all the Mobeetie evidence be disallowed and that the conspiracy charges be thrown out. Semaan restated the promise made by the United States attorney in Amarillo. Failing to honor that promise, he said, would represent a serious breach of faith and fairness. Two witnesses had been subpoenaed to testify, United States attorney Robert Travis of Fort Worth and Pat Mulloy, United States attorney for the Northern District of Texas. Both government attorneys agreed that the promise had been made.

When Mulloy took the stand, however, he made one important clarification. The promise that no further charges would be filed related to that case applied only to the Northern District of Texas. This trial, he pointed out, was in the Western District of Texas.

The motion was denied.

IN THE LAST MONTH OF THE trial, the defection of a gang moll took center stage in the drama. From her motel room in Del Rio, Joan Taylor faithfully wrote love notes to James, sometimes several times a day, asking if he received the toothpaste she'd sent; giving updates on their dogs, Shalimar and Gigi; and pledging her undying loyalty. Over the weekend break in the third week of March, she had a heart-to-heart talk with the FBI and the United States attorney. By the time the trial convened in El Paso in April, her case had been severed. She was now a government informer and witness.

Betty Joyce Dabbs, alias Joan Taylor, with Shalimar. *Courtesy of Debi Dabbs.*

During the first two months of the trial, she had insisted that, as James's common-law wife, she should be addressed as Joan Taylor James. Now she said her name was Betty Joyce Dabbs.

When Betty/Joan took the witness stand in El Paso, she admitted that she was a prostitute and that James was a professional bank burglar. "That's all he ever did," she said.[195]

She also told how the boys fenced traveler's checks and other financial instruments through Joseph Spagnoli, a convicted forger and mafia character in Chicago. It appears that the FBI suspected that the Overton/James gang had been laundering traveler's checks and other hot paper through Spagnoli since 1962.[196]

The transactions with Spagnoli were number sixteen on the government's list of separate offenses committed by the conspiracy, and another brief named Spagnoli as an unindicted co-conspirator. In the beginning, he was also on the list of government witnesses, but he did not appear, and it's too bad because his involvement with the Texans suggests an additional layer of organized crime activities, even, believe it or not, possible links to Kennedy assassination conspiracies.[197] (For a summary of other tenuous links to the JFK assassination, see Appendix 1.)

A native Chicagoan and professional gambler, Spagnoli would have cut an interesting figure in the El Paso courtroom, had he appeared. At the time, he was serving a fifteen-year sentence on a 1965 conviction for counterfeiting United States Savings Bonds. A Secret Service agent named Abraham Bolden had been convicted of bribery in the same case.[198] Bolden, the first African American on the White House detail, claimed that he was a victim of racism because he had offered to tell the Warren Commission about drunkenness and negligence in the White House detail prior to the Kennedy assassination.

Although Spagnoli turned government witness in the bribery case, he claimed that he'd been pressured to commit perjury and that he was innocent of the counterfeiting charges. Or, as Spagnoli put it, "I'm innocent to them charges. I didn't conspire with nobody. I don't have to have a deal. I don't need no deal. I am innocent of them charges. I didn't do none of them things."

Tim Overton, guilty. *Courtesy of the NARA.*

Betty/Joan's defection provided the prosecution with a much-needed boost, even though her testimony was later contradicted on several points and even helped gain an acquittal for one, possibly two other, defendants. The media played up the sexual content of her testimony, with salacious quotes about a ménage à trois in Chicago and other aspects of her profession.[199]

Compared to modern-day sitcom dialogue, rappers and shock jocks, it was all pretty tame stuff, and today, the thing people remember best is Overton and Cathey shagging each other in the jail cell in Del Rio. Maybe it's because it basically sums up the thugs' attitude toward the Big Circus. As Betty King said, "They just didn't care."

In El Paso on June 13, the defense rested without calling a single witness. The case had been fought and lost on motions. The defense counsel, down to seven lawyers, was burned out.

Judge Suttle urged Morgan to cut his losses. Four more acquittals were announced: Travis Erwin and Darrell Overton were finally cut loose, as were Judy Cathey and Elizabeth Sherman, the first women to be shown mercy in the case. On the afternoon of May 13, Mildred Green had a seizure in court. Mildred—or Dee Dee, as she was known—the girlfriend of Darrell Overton, worked at Tanna Wallace's bordello outside San Antonio, which was adjacent to a breeder of Shetland horses and poodles, hence the name Pony and Poodle Farm, and the alternate Texas Cowboy Dog Kennels. On Saturdays, Freddie Semaan drove out to collect Green's earnings, applying them to Darrell's legal bills.[200]

According to medical records, when Green was a child, her grandmother subjected her to bizarre taunts, such as "you're only half a woman" and "pretty is as pretty does."[201] She began dating boys in seventh grade, after which her grades tanked. At age fourteen, she married an army private and took a job in a beauty shop.

Four years later, she was admitted to a hospital in hysterics. "They threw my babies in the trash can," she screamed. Now eighteen, she'd been hospitalized for three tubal pregnancies (the first one in the eighth grade), a miscarriage and a complete hysterectomy. After a brief stay at Austin State Hospital, Darrell Overton caught her on the rebound and turned her out.

Despite having files pertaining to all the above, Ernest Morgan suspected that Green's breakdown might be a clever bit of playacting. Preferring to err on the side of caution, if not humanity, Judge Suttle issued an order that Green's case be temporarily set aside.

Ten defendants remained: Tim Overton, Jerry Ray James, Hank Bowen, Chester Schutz, Freddie Hedges, Curt Garrett, Ben Tisdale, Dale Hall, Sue Overton and Mary Farmer. Fewer defendants, however, did not necessarily mean smooth sailing. Their moods varied from day to day, depending on what drugs they'd been able to obtain. During the first week in June, the men staged a sit-out, jamming a bench behind the cell door so it couldn't be opened. Tear gas canisters brought about their surrender. Later, Tim Overton got into an argument with Dale Hall, and a mêlée ensued in the tight quarters of the cell. Fifteen police officers were dispatched to quell what the newspapers called "a riot." When the judge asked Hall how his leg came to be broken, he said he'd fallen from a bench.[202]

MORGAN ARGUED STRENUOUSLY AGAINST acquitting any of the women. The government, he believed, could not and should not let go of the prostitution part of the conspiracy indictment.

Week after week, jurors and spectators saw the women in court, often looking haggard from working overtime to help pay legal expenses for their men. A week after Green's seizure, Cathey experienced a recurrence of an excruciatingly painful female disorder. During a hearing outside the presence of the jury, attorney Max Flusche asked the judge to excuse Cathey from the day's proceedings because of illness. Judge Suttle was a hard sell, saying, "In other words, she wants some dope...I have sat here with severe sinus headaches and managed to stay going." He finally relented, and the trial was recessed for five days.[203]

Hank Bowen, guilty. *Courtesy of the NARA.*

Betty King told me she worked at the Chicken Ranch in La Grange for the duration of the trial. "The lawyer was expensive," she said, "but I was happy to be far away from there because they were trying to send everybody they could to prison."[204]

When the case went to the jury during the third week of June, the jurors rejected the prostitution charge. Sue Overton and Mary Farmer were acquitted. Never mind that Farmer drove the getaway car in Pond Creek and Overton had been associated with Tim Overton over the course of scores of felonious adventures. After the adjournment, charges against Mildred Green were dropped. Despite stubborn arguments against it from Ernest Morgan, Suttle wasn't having any. Maybe his head cold had cleared up.

Curt Garrett and Fred Hedges were acquitted. Tim Overton, Jerry Ray James, Chester Schutz, Dale Hall and Ben Tisdale were convicted on all bank burglary–related counts and sentenced to five years in prison, the maximum.

After four months of being under a gag order from the court, Fred Semaan was free to blow off steam with reporters, many of whom had chafed under Suttle's restrictions on press coverage. Semaan told reporters that the government had spent

William Brown, charges dismissed. *Courtesy of the NARA.*

roughly $1.5 million on the case and that six convictions out of twenty in the original indictment was a poor return on the investment.[205]

For his part, Judge Suttle confined his comments to the size of the trial, stating that it was the longest in Texas history. By most measures, the Overton/James trial even eclipsed the 1963 swindling trial—which was held in the same courtroom—of LBJ crony and conman Bill Sol Estes. That one lasted only two days, and the conviction was overturned on appeal, but Estes got the cover of *Time*.[206]

# 9
# THE BIG FREEZE OUT: 1972

*One day when we were kids, eleven or twelve, I guess, I was walking home from*
*school and I walked past this place, this house that used to be downtown, a whore*
*house. Tim was standing there in the doorway. I said, "What're you doing here?"*
*He said, "I'm the straw boss. I'm the big man here."*
—*Pete Johnson*[207]

Starting over can be difficult, especially when you've been away, but Tim Overton had a plan. In the spring of 1971, in his final sentencing hearing (delayed because of a judicial error), Overton told Judge Suttle that his uncle, an ironworker in Anchorage, Alaska, had a job waiting for him. Anchorage is a long way from Austin, but that was the idea. "I intend to leave Texas," he said, "because I feel that my reputation and what have you wouldn't allow me to live there."[208]

At Leavenworth, Overton was busy with track, handball, baseball and college courses, activities that, he said, helped keep his negative energies in check. He was sorry for his behavior in Del Rio and El Paso. "In the past I've had a bad temper and I let it get the best of me," he said. "I feel like now possibly I may have been able to overcome this problem."

Once he got himself established, he hoped to get into the computer field.

Suttle congratulated Overton on his rehabilitation. "The court has always been aware of your intelligence and potential," said the judge. "It's just unfortunate that you got off in a bad area."

Wherever Overton went after he left Leavenworth, it wouldn't be with the former Mrs. Sue Overton. She was in San Antonio now, married to Jack L. Odom. An ex-football player for Ole Miss (1947 to '48) and former air force staff sergeant during the Korean War, Odom owned several topless clubs that catered to the Alamo City's large population of military personnel. Probably the best known of these was at the Sidewinder a-Go-Go on Highway 90 across from Lackland Air Force Base. Odom was well fixed in San Antonio, and with his protection, Sue wasn't as fearful about Overton being released from prison.[209]

Sue Odom wasn't the only one looking over her shoulder these days. By 1970, involvement in the Dixie Mafia meant stepping over a lot of blood puddles, a fact that was underscored repeatedly in the "Dixie Mafia Intelligence Report," compiled by the Kansas attorney general's office in 1974.[210] At least five (and probably several more) characters who were close to Tim Overton were murdered between 1969 and '70: Carl Douglas White, Donald Lester James, Sonny Stanley, George Albert McGann and Betty Joyce Askins.

Still living fast in the '70s: Judy Cathey, second from left, back row. Her brother, James Bill "Jimbo" Lawler, second from right. *Courtesy of Laylee Muslovski.*

JUDY CATHEY WASN'T GOING TO Alaska, either. She married a man named Harper and moved to Houston, but not necessarily with him. Although Cathey and Overton were no longer together, Overton still maintained a relationship with members of Cathey's extended family. As Laylee Muslovski put it, they "looked after Tim's business while he was gone." At the time, Muslovski was too young to fully comprehend what her uncles and cousins were up to. Years later, she started asking questions. Her cousin told her that "after Tim came back from Leavenworth, he brought over a huge bag of money...as payment for taking care of things."[211]

After the conspiracy trial, the woman formerly known as Joan Dobbs Taylor moved to Oklahoma City, where, through marriage, her legal name became Betty Joyce Askins. Her new husband, Jess Bartlett Askins, was handsome, thirty years old and—as a co-owner in his father's bail bonds company, real estate business and oil investments—quite wealthy.[212]

In an Austin motel room on April 16, 1969, Betty shot Jess during a marital spat. He survived and declined to press charges.[213] On November 4, 1970, in the family home in Oklahoma City, another argument ended with gunfire. Jess was drunk, waving a .38 pistol around the bedroom. Betty was on her knees, begging, "Don't do it. It's cocked." He called the housekeeper and said, "Get her out of here." The housekeeper was helping Betty to her feet when Jess shot Betty in the face, and she fell dead, "as if she had fainted."[214]

Askins pleaded guilty to manslaughter. Reporting in the *Oklahoman* was laced with terse irony. When Askins languished in jail until his trial in January, the headline was "Bond Denied Professional Bail Maker."[215] When, during his third year in prison, he petitioned for permission to marry his lawyer, Joann Fisher Corrigan, "Wife Killer Asks to Marry Lawyer" said it all.[216]

TIM OVERTON WAS DISCHARGED FROM federal custody on October 8, 1972, after serving a total of five years and four months. He didn't go to Alaska. He had a girlfriend in East Dallas, an apartment in Fort Worth and, in Austin, he rented space at a place called Rocket Square. The south-facing end of the block at Fifteenth and Lavaca Streets was home to apartments, restaurants, Eli the Tailor (who ran a little policy operation on the side), a travel agency and other entities.[217]

Charles Craig and his brother Gary had gone to high school with Overton. After graduation, the brothers attended UT and became lawyers.

"One day we were walking down Fifteenth Street and this voice called out, 'Hey Gary!' and it was Timmy," said Charles. "He'd just gotten out of

Tim, probably fourteen or fifteen. This picture is one of the keepsakes he left in the care of Kay Beasley. *Courtesy of Kay Beasley.*

Leavenworth. He's all smiles and he says, 'I just rented an office in this building.' We asked him what he was doing, what kind of business was he in? He said, 'I'm gonna take over this town, man. I'm taking over.'"

"He looked real good after he got out," said Betty King. "He had slimmed down, and he had new clothes and stuff." King was living in Fort Worth and working as a nurse's aid in Dallas.

"My roommate brought him home one night to see me," said King. "We used to hang out at this dive in East Dallas. We knew the couple who owned the place, but I can't remember their names. Tim ended up giving me all these family photos and stuff. He just had this crazed feeling about family photographs. They just were very, very important to him."

Back in high school, a lifetime ago, Overton had given a bundle of photos and other memorabilia to his girlfriend, Kay Beasley. She didn't think about it again until 2009, when she unpacked a box of high school yearbooks from her mother's attic. The photos turned over to King were lost in a fire.

ON FRIDAY NIGHT, DECEMBER 9, an arctic front blasted through Texas. The *Statesman* called it "an icy shroud." Betty King had planned to meet up with Overton and their friends at the bar, but she ended up working. Sometime after midnight, Overton went to see his girlfriend, Wanda Jewel Long. She lived at an apartment in East Dallas next to a sprawling greenbelt called Fair Oaks Park. Long was twenty-eight years old, with a record for prostitution.

At 3:05 a.m., a park ranger found Overton face down in the apartment parking lot. He'd been shot twice in the back and twice in the back of the head with a .45 automatic. His boots were gone, but $300 in cash and a little black book were inside his overcoat. A hit man leaves cash on the victim to send a message that it wasn't about the money.

Around sunrise, a passing motorist saw Wanda Long's crumpled form in the snow behind some trees about a mile from where Overton was killed. She'd been shot in the back of the head. Knots of frosted hair and skull fragments marked the path between the body and the road. Five neatly folded twenties were in her coat.

According to the murder file, both victims were shot inside a car in the apartment parking lot. Apparently, the killing started out clever but turned messy. Witnesses reported seeing someone before dawn at a nearby carwash, hosing out a silver/gray 1973 Pontiac—an odd sight on the night of an icestorm.[218]

The Dallas Police Department was stingy with information. The murders appeared to be connected, they said. Robbery was probably not the motive.

After the initial big scoop in the *Statesman* ("Local 1960's Crime Figure Shot Dead"), most of the media seemed to lose interest.[219] Time passed, no breaks in the case were announced. Even "Austin Underworld of the '60s: Overton Gang Recalled," written four years later, seemed to suggest that the crime remained unsolved.

> *Police believed Overton had gone back to his old habit of robbing dice and poker games, as he reportedly had done in Austin in the 1960s. He tried to take over vice operations headed by others on various occasions.*[220]

What the article suggests is that Overton had gone out sticking up gamblers, lone-wolf style; somebody got mad and plugged him. While true that robbing games used to be part of the gang's portfolio of mischief, they did it as a crew, with coordination and planning. Nat Henderson, who wrote the piece, certainly knew better. And Overton's attempts to "take over vice operations headed by others" was something Henderson knew about and could have elaborated on. Too bad he didn't.

Overton had said "I'm taking over" so many times, it could have been carved on his grave marker. Instead, the marker bears the generic sentiment "Gone but not forgotten." I was reminded of Pete Johnson's story of when they were a couple of adolescent kids, eleven or twelve years old. One day Johnson was surprised to see Overton standing in the entrance to a bordello. "I'm the straw boss here," Overton said. "I'm the big man in this place." Similarly, "I'm taking over this town" could've been a reflexive joke or a quote from a dozen gangster films—or not.[221]

A lot of people in Austin had theories about why Tim Overton was killed. For a while, I kept a list of them, but the whole thing never felt right to me, so I went to a reliable authority: Eddie Wilson.

"Little Larry did it," said Wilson. "Little Larry was mean, rotten, a little guy with a little guy complex."[222] Wilson knew people who knew people. He'd heard the usual theories, including one that the Dallas crime lords ordered the hit and Dallas police said "nice work," but he suggested we ask Ed Wendler.

We went to see Wendler in Lockhart, where he was living around the corner from our favorite barbecue joint. "It was a paid hit," Wendler said, sounding almost bitter about it. "It wasn't over some game that got robbed. The people that will kill you are the people who have a drug ring or a poker syndicate or whores, that's an ongoing business for them and they're sheltered back from it...They wanted him out of there. Tim was beginning to be big enough that he was a thorn in their side, so they killed him."

Wendler might have known who "they" were but didn't say. He'd been a fixture in Austin's back rooms and smoky corridors for decades. He died in March 2004 before I got another chance to ask.

On a careful rereading of *Dirty Dealing*, I found a few references to Larry Culbreath and Tim Overton and a few false notes in an otherwise superb book. Author Gary Cartwright writes that "Little Larry Culbreath was a San Antonio tough who used to run with the infamous Overton gang of Austin, until he was convicted of the contract killing of Timmie [SIC] Overton." Larry Culbreath was from Austin, a contemporary of Tim Overton and had known him at least as far back as junior high school. They were in the same class at Stephen F. Austin High School until Little Larry dropped out. But I've never seen any reliable information about Little Larry being part of Overton's crews of burglars and car dealers prior to 1972. Maybe it happened, but I doubt it.[223]

Little Larry Culbreath was well connected in the gambling world—as in Dallas, Fort Worth, San Antonio and Las Vegas. According to "Dixie Mafia Intelligence Report," commissioned by the Kansas state attorney general and published in 1974, Little Larry was "one of the more efficient up-and-coming Dixie Mafia hit men" jockeying for a leadership role.[224]

On April 27, 1973, Little Larry was pulled over in Decatur, Georgia, while driving with expired plates.[225] Dallas County filed extradition papers, and he was returned to Texas to face charges on the double slaying. No court-

Walter Webb Hall in 2004, built as the home of the 40 Acres Club in 1962, a playhouse for UT alumni and their supporters. *Author's collection.*

appointed attorney was good enough for this deal: Charles W. Tessmer was hired to steer the defense team. A profile of Tessmer in the *Dallas Observer* referred to him as "the don of Dallas criminal attorneys."[226] Maybe Little Larry really did have "up-and-coming Dixie Mafia hit man" credentials. Assisting Tessmer were Dallas attorneys Frank S. Wright and Ronald L. Goranson and Bob Hendricks of McKinney, a recently elected member of the Texas legislature.

D.J. Driscoll, a prosecutor under Dallas County district attorney Henry Wade, handled the prosecution. Judge Thomas B. Thorpe, appointed to the 203rd Criminal District Court in 1973, tried the case. The file is three-quarters of an inch thick. At Lake Ray Hubbard, an impoundment on the East Fork of the Trinity River a short drive from East Dallas, eyewitnesses spotted the 1973 Pontiac, which was registered to Little Larry's mother, Cleo Culbreath. Forensic evidence was abundant (bloody floor mats, cigarette butts, shell casings, guns and unburned items from a pile of ashes at Lake Ray Hubbard: Overton's boots and Long's hair brush, drivers license and purse). But for all the legal tricks pulled by Tessmer and his team, you'd think they expected a complete exoneration and a letter of apology from Dallas.

After numerous delays and continuances, a trial date was set for November 8, 1974, but at the eleventh hour, the defense cut a deal. Little Larry confessed to the two murders, pleaded guilty and received conviction on both counts, and Judge Thorpe gave him ten years of probation. I went back through the file to see if I'd missed something, but there was no explanation for it: two people, shot in the back of the head, ten years probation.

CHARLES CRAIG TOLD ME THAT Overton had another scheme for getting revenge on Darrell Royal and UT and that Little Larry was his partner on the deal. "They were going to break into the Forty Acres Club and steal all the art," he said.

A '60s modern structure at Twenty-fifth and Guadalupe Streets, the Forty Acres Club was founded by fat cat alumni as an all-white preserve in 1962. In August 1972, just before Overton made parole, the club was sold. There was talk of a faculty club taking it over, but the details were up in the air.[227]

"Before they pulled the heist, Larry went to Fort Worth and talked to the people there," said Craig. "Larry told them, I can do the job without Tim, just cut him out of the deal and you can deal with me directly."

The Fort Worth cats liked that idea, but they wanted one more thing. "They wanted Larry to kill Timmy, too," said Craig. "The pimps up there had it in for the Overtons, you know, ever since Darrell killed that pimp up there [Curtis Newsom] and he had friends there. So Larry killed him."

No mention of a burglary at the location was found in the *Statesman* or *Daily Texan* between late 1972 and early 1973. Apparently, it didn't happen. Today, the building is known as Walter Webb Hall. The one remaining piece of original art is the Paul Hatgil mosaic mural of the university's Main Building, as the original Victorian-Gothic structure looked in 1899. The artwork is mortared to the wall in a reception area, and although it probably wouldn't be much tougher than peeling a vault or drilling a cannonball safe, there it remains today.

BETWEEN 1970 AND '73, SEVERAL dynamics in the Dallas–Fort Worth area came together to cause the FBI special concern, including a new incoming mafia boss (Joseph Campisi, replacing Joe Civello, who died in 1970), the first new Dallas County sheriff since the Bonnie and Clyde era (Clarence Jones, after the 1970 death of James Eric "Bill" Decker) and possible new moves by the New Orleans mafia boss Carlos Marcello. In the flurry of FBI reports from that era, I found this half-page memo from Special Agent Ronald K. Jannings in Fort Worth:

> *On June 5, 1973, RITA FISHER, Tarrant County Organized Crime Unit, advised that Telephone Number 731-3035 listed to W.R. PATTERSON, 6503 Plaza Parkway, Apartment Number 204, had been used in the bookmaking operation of SAM BENSON and FREDDIE CLINTON HEDGES from November 15, 1972 through December 4, 1972. FISHER advised that there is an indication that LARRY CULBREATH and FREDDIE CLINTON HEDGES attempted to take over or would take over SAM BENSON's book sometime in December 1972. CULBREATH has since been arrested for the murder of TIM OVERTON and OVERTON's girlfriend in a gangland type slaying in Dallas, Texas.*[228]

Various sources told me that the FBI questioned Freddie Hedges about the murders of December 9, 1972. This paragraph offers an explanation. Sam "Lightning" Benson was a well-known Dallas bookie. His name appears in other FBI reports I've seen concerning another Dallas playmate of Tim Overton and the guys, the seemingly indestructible R.D. Matthews.

IT TURNS OUT THAT JUDGE Thomas B. Thorpe wasn't the only party who heard Little Larry Culbreath's confession to the Overton-Long murders.

Sometime after December 9, 1972, Little Larry came by to visit Sue and Jack Odom at the Sidewinder A-Go-Go.

"He bragged to my mom," said the youngest daughter of Sue Overton. "He told her, he said, 'Sue, you should've seen that motherfucker. I scattered his brains all over the place.'"[229]

Sue Odom wasn't the only person who heard the story from Little Larry himself. An anonymous gambler we'll call Jack Wild, not a person who is easily shocked, remembered breaking out in goose bumps when Little Larry gave his account at an Austin bar: "Larry just started telling us what happened. He said that Tim and the girl begged for their lives. Tim was crying. The girl asked for a chance to make her peace with the Lord and Larry let her and then shot her. He related the story very coldly, very unemotionally and it chilled everybody when they heard it."

The brain-splatter confession was also unspooled at a church gathering. Whether the killer was seeking forgiveness or trying to impress certain unnamed deities was not clear.[230]

"TIM AND FAT JERRY HAD just run crazy all over the country for years," said Betty King. "Tim had been in for five years and other people had already stepped into his shoes, and they weren't going to allow him to come take over again. So they just decided to kill him."

She told me she believes that the hit was a "joint venture" involving some of their mutual friends at the dive bar in East Dallas. Later on, she went back to the bar and asked questions. "I said, 'Had I been there, would you have killed me?' They said, 'Well, we don't know.'"

She didn't have much to say about Larry Culbreath. "I met him at the bar, but I never knew him."

I was curious about that bar and the people who owned it, but I didn't have much to go on. I bugged King, but she said she just couldn't remember. One day I was looking through a folder labeled "Dead Overtons" and found the answer. I e-mailed King and asked: "Was it Dale and Winnie Hall?"

She wrote back: "Yes."

The headline in the *Dallas Morning News*, "Police Seek Connection in Death, Visit to DA," told most of the story: "Dale Norwood Hall, 51, was found shot through the head in the front seat of his wife's automobile parked in his driveway at 6140 Richmond early Friday." Hall had visited Dallas County district attorney Henry Wade "hours before his death" on March 2, 1973.[231]

Dallas police said that a pistol was found in his lap and a note on the car seat. Handwriting analysis and other tests were pending. The article mentioned

Hall's connection with Tim Overton, identified as "an underworld figure…a member of a gang with ties to the Fort Worth underworld."

"Police said Hall had been with Overton the night before" the Overton/ Long murders. Homicide detectives interviewed Hall two days later "but reportedly learned nothing significant." Then, not quite two months later, Dale Hall went to see the district attorney. That night, someone shot him in the head.

The death certificate, filed on March 5, 1973, gives Hall's occupation as "lounge operator" and the cause of death as "self-inflicted gunshot wound."[232]

Overton was murdered exactly two months after his parole, less than two years after appearing at the final sentencing where he spoke with such apparent sincerity about rehabilitation, getting a degree and maybe going into the computer field. As George Phifer, the first cop I spoke with about this book, told me, "Tim was a likeable fellow, but he was always trying to con you. He had no conscience. He was a sociopath."

He didn't go to Alaska. The Big Freeze came to him.

# 10

# AUSTIN WEIRD

Hattie Valdes died on February 19, 1976, at the age of seventy-two. Her last will bequeathed large sums to various charities, a nephew, former employees and her yardman, but the bulk of her considerable estate was left to her adopted daughter, Betty Jean Valdes, a sister of the Holy Cross in South Bend, Indiana.[233] Her friends, bankers and lawyers had long known of her generosity, and her last testament proved that she was more than just a whorehouse madam and soft target for thieves and cops.

The death of Hattie Valdes must have seemed like the end of an era, but many of the old anachronisms from the Austin underworld refused to stay dead or go quietly. This was evidenced, of course, by the gangland slaying of Tim Overton's former cohort, Travis Schnautz, on August 12, 1976. This killing served as a catalyst for some of the events that happened later, such as the *Statesman*'s exposé on massage parlors in Austin, but some resurrections of '60s thug culture probably would have surfaced anyway.

In May 1976, for example, a headline in the *San Antonio Express-News*, "Massive Dope Ring Back in Action," chronicled the latest chapter in the outlaw career of John W. "Webbie" Flanagan, who had been convicted of tax evasion and disbarred in 1972, was now utilizing his skills as a bush pilot with a drug smuggling ring.[234] He achieved almost mythic status during the cocaine cowboy era of the dope racket in Texas. After several convictions on federal charges and short sentences, he finished a fifteen-year sentence around the year 2000. Now in his eighties, he appears to have given up the outlaw life.

About two weeks after the gangland killings of August 1976, Charles Ray Overton came rolling into town, not in a Dixie Mafia Cadillac but in a Woodstock-era caravan. He was shaggy haired and bearded, with a wife called Boom Boom and a total of five children and stepchildren.[235] Released from federal prison in 1974 (his habitual criminal conviction had been overturned), he was driving a psychedelicized 1959 GM school bus with "Fundamental Church for the Study of Absolute Reality" painted on the sides and a big, drooping crucifix on the front grille.

Here's a flashback of my own: I remember seeing that bus parked at the corner of East Riverside and Manlove Streets, in front of some old frame houses. That's where they lived.

Charles Ray Overton's arrival was heralded with a *Statesman* article, "Overton Gang Member Gives Up Life of Crime for Religion"); a startling photo; and a caption studded with cosmic names—"Ready" Overton, Boom Boom, an infant named Magic Marc, a daughter named O'Joy, etc. Their livelihood came from sign painting and odd jobs. For many years, he also had a used tire store on East First Street called O'Joy. It's a tight family when the father names a tire store after his daughter.

The former Magic Marc contacted me and shared information, but his father, he said, regretted his outlaw past and did not want to talk to me. Marc, who has a different last name now, has a successful career in the technology industry. His father died in 2007.

On his release from prison, Darrell Overton married and adopted two children. He worked as a construction surveyor and later ran a junk store. He continued to struggle with addiction and died in 2003. William John Overton graduated UT with a degree in engineering and became a successful civil engineer. Finus Ewil Overton Jr. is apparently still living. We had one brief contact.

One of the gaudiest flashbacks to Overton gang craziness took place from the fall of 1976 through early 1977. A feud between ex-Overton associate Frank H. Smith and Isaac Rabb over control of the Austin auto salvage business broke into the open after an armed robbery attempt at Rabb's salvage yard, masterminded by Smith, failed miserably, resulting in the death of one monster mask–wearing, near-sighted gunman. The investigation and subsequent criminal trial laid bare other incidents of vice, sleaze and mayhem. Walk-on roles in the parade of pulp nonfiction featured Chester Schutz, Curtis Garrett and other veterans of the Overton era.

Junkyard wars are probably too low-brow even for Quentin Tarantino to spin into cinematic gold, but it remains a mystery why the director of *Reservoir*

*Dogs*, *Pulp Fiction* and *Kill Bill* hasn't purchased an option on a version of the Jerry Ray James story, especially given the filmmaker's fondness for the '70s period.[236] Perhaps it's because some aspects of Fat Jerry's crime career would require too great a suspension of belief, even for viewers who may have migrated to crime cinema via *Grand Theft Auto*.

Let's begin, for example, on October 18, 1976, with the highly unusual judicial decision to parole James to the custody of A.B. Munson, a former New Mexico State Police major who was now a civilian. Exactly one week later, James and some friends pulled a brutal home invasion robbery that scored $240,000 in jewelry. This crime set the pattern for some fifteen other armed robberies committed during the next few months. James may or may not have been involved in all of them.

Convicted the following June, James was slapped with two life sentences and transferred to New Mexico State Penitentiary, a facility that burned down in February 1980 during one of the worst prison riots in United States history.[237] Thirty-two inmates were killed, many of them raped with axe handles and blow-torched to death for being informants.

Jerry Ray James bragged about being one of the ringleaders of the riot and killings.

STRANGELY ENOUGH, SOME BRIGHT minds at the United States Department of Justice conceived a plan to offer James a pardon, a place in the witness protection program and a payment of $250,000. Our government wanted this violent, serial offender's assistance in obtaining a conviction in what the FBI called "the crime of the century"—the assassination of federal district judge John H. Wood Jr.

The judge, who had acquired the nicknamed "Maximum John" for his habit of handing down harsh sentences for drug offenders, was killed with a single shot by a powerful rifle as he left his home in San Antonio on May 29, 1979. It was the first murder of a federal judge in one hundred years and the biggest federal investigation since the Kennedy assassination.

The alleged purchaser of the hit was Jimmy Chagra, a major drug smuggler from El Paso. Chagra was originally scheduled to be tried before Judge Wood's court on May 29, 1979. After an inside source informed Chagra that the judge intended to sentence him to life without parole, he offered a hit man $250,000 to kill the judge.

Charles V. Harrelson—a contract killer, gambler and the father of actor Woody Harrelson—was arrested and convicted of killing Wood and sentenced to life. Two others were also convicted for their roles in the plot:

Jimmy Chagra's wife, Elizabeth, and his brother, Joe. Convicting Jimmy Chagra of hiring Charles Harrelson proved problematic for various reasons, however, and in desperation, the feds turned to Jerry Ray James.

To claim his prize package, James was expected to get close to Chagra, get him on tape admitting that he hired Charles Harrelson to kill Judge Wood and then testify about it in court. James was transferred to Leavenworth, where he became Chagra's cellmate, gained his trust and got him to talk about hiring Charles Harrelson to kill Judge Wood for $250,000—on tape.

In February 1983, in a federal courtroom in Florida, James took the stand and repeated what Chagra had told him.[238]

Unfortunately for the prosecution, the jury panel wasn't impressed with the late Tim Overton's running buddy. Chagra's attorney, Oscar Goodman (prior to being elected mayor of Las Vegas for three terms, 1999 to 2011), blasted holes in portions of James's testimony and shamed the government for making such a cynical deal for his testimony. Goodman possessed a keen ability to sniff out cynical deals, having earned the appellation "mob lawyer" by representing men such as Meyer Lansky, Nicky Scarfo, Frank "Lefty" Rosenthal and Anthony "Tony the Ant" Spilotro. The Florida jury panel rejected the murder charge but voted to convict Chagra on three lesser charges, which added another fifteen years to his sentence. Later, in a plea bargain, Chagra admitted that he had hired Harrelson and also confessed to the attempted murder of a United States attorney.

It's unknown whether Jerry Ray James got the full $250,000 or not, but he did get his freedom.[239] Debi Dabbs told me that when she saw him in 1983, she almost didn't recognize him. "His hair and beard had turned white," she said. "He seemed to have shrunk, too. He looked like a little old Santa Claus."[240]

SPEAKING OF MERRY LITTLE ELVES, Little Larry Culbreath also emerged from the crime of the century in reasonably good condition. He even had good luck with his probation judge. Back in April 21, 1976, the terms of his probation had been modified to allow travel between Atascosa County (the location of the Culbreath family farm) and Austin "while caring for the needs of his mother."[241] Maybe she wanted her car back.

On May 20, Little Larry was charged with violating the federal firearms act and convicted in September, with no apparent infringement on his freedom.[242]

On October 13, 1978, according to Atascosa County sheriff Tommy Williams, Little Larry reported finding a downed Cessna 310 aircraft on a ranch where he was working. A total of seven hundred pounds of marijuana was recovered from the plane. Williams praised Little Larry

Eddie Wilson, imagineering the 1970s and beyond at the epic music hall he founded and heroically operated, Armadillo World Headquarters. *Photo by Van Brooks, courtesy of Eddie Wilson.*

in a letter to Judge Thorpe, also enclosing a clipping from the *Pleasanton Express* about the discovery of the dope smuggler's aircraft by "an excited West Atascosa rancher."

Seeking respite from their civic duties no doubt, on January 11, 1979, Little Larry, a male companion and two Las Vegas women rented a cabin at a coastal resort in Rockport, Texas, called the Sea Gun.[243] Another man joined the group later. According to one hotel employee, one of Little Larry's companions looked a lot like Charles Harrelson. The party did some high-stakes gambling and made ninety-four long-distance calls, many of them to gambling casinos in Las Vegas. With the Super Bowl about a week away, it was a busy time for bookmakers. On January 17, after getting word that a sheriff's raiding party was on its way, they disappeared, leaving behind a sex toy, a dog cage, gambling paraphernalia, gambling slips (some with figures as high as $500,000 written on them), a battery-powered TV set and all the clothes they weren't wearing when they split.

Later, during the investigation of the killing of Judge John Wood, the FBI noted that the judge and his family were staying at their place on Key Allegro, just across the bay, simultaneous with the Culbreath party's Sea Gun stay. The latter had also rented a boat to take them over to Key Allegro on three successive days.[244] Did Little Larry and friends go to the coast to gamble and hook some redfish or to keep tabs on Judge Wood, study his movements and case the kill?

The full facts have never been made public, but Little Larry had already been questioned by G-men. The interview took place the day after the murder, when, it so happened, Little Larry was driving Harrelson's car. Later, at a poker game, Little Larry bragged that he knew who killed Wood. In several of the FBI's recorded conversations about the killing of Judge Wood, Jimmy Chagra says, "Maybe Little Larry did it." It's not clear if it was supposed to be a joke or not, and if so, why would that be funny?[245]

On May 8, 1979, less than four months after the stakeout party at the Sea Gun, Judge Thomas B. Thorp of Dallas reduced Little Larry's term of probation for killing Tim Overton and Wanda Long from ten years to four and a half. The verdict was set aside, the indictment dismissed and Little Larry was free to go.

What the hell, he's probably done worse things.[246]

# The Overtons in JFK Conspiracyland

Dallas, forever infamous as the place that killed Kennedy, and its adjacent Cowtown cousin, the equally mobbed-up Fort Worth, were regular playgrounds for Tim Overton until he got killed there. I think it's a testament to the vitality of the Dallas/Fort Worth underworld that so many theories have also circulated to explain the contract killing of Tim Overton. What was a haven for gamblers, pimps, thieves and killers in the '60s and '70s continues to be a rich mine of material for conspiracy buffs and true crime aficionados today.

*The Cold Six Thousand*, by James Ellroy, is one of many fictional treatments of the notion that rogue government agents and organized crime figures conspired to kill JFK. Although fictional, the novel is richly informed by historical research. Ellroy sifted through many of the same FBI files cited in this book. Other well-known variations of the government/mob theory include *Crossfire: The Plot that Killed Kennedy*, by Jim Marrs, and the fictional political thriller *JFK*, whose screenplay was largely adapted from *Crossfire* by filmmaker Oliver Stone.

FBI files on various members of the Overton/James gang are voluminous, running to hundreds of pages. One particular document, which happens to be included in the President John F. Kennedy Assassination Records Collection, helps chronicle the involvement of the Overton crowd in the Dallas and Fort Worth underworld during the period before and after the assassination.[247]

"Crime Conditions in the Dallas Division," dated September 15, 1964, originally ran over sixty pages, of which only twenty-two redacted pages have been made public. A cover memo offers excuses for the agency's slack attention to organized crime in the area, citing the drain on FBI resources and manpower due to the Kennedy assassination. The good news, more or less, was that six new investigations had been opened since March 1, 1964.[248]

A list of fourteen names, "Gamblers and Bookmakers Still Known to Operate in Fort Worth," includes three Austinites: James Timothy Overton, Chester Arthur Schutz Jr. and Clifford Henry Bowen. They're identified as "bookmakers [and] gamblers [who specialize] in dice hustling, dice switching and as card sharps." This confirms that the Overtons were around and active at the same time as Jack Ruby, R.D. Matthews, Carlos Marcello, Joseph Frank Civello, Joseph Campisi and other individuals frequently mentioned in government/mob conspiracy theories.

The description of the protocols pertaining to four of the fourteen fits protocols that have elsewhere been ascribed to members of the Overton group:

> *It has been ascertained that any of this latter group will go anyplace in the United States where a "sucker" has been set up and in some instances they have been called in by "home town gamblers" to "chill" some person who has gotten lucky and is beating the house. Each man is considered an expert in his individual field either being a dice hustler or a card sharp* [or] *an organizer* [who] *can stay in the background and out of direct contact with the "sucker."*

Under the heading "IV. Notorious Places of Amusement and Criminal Hangouts," number one on the list is the Egyptian Lounge in Dallas, a restaurant founded by Joseph Campisi after World War II that was a magnet for gamblers, bookies and characters. Campisi's son, Joseph, was prominent in the Dallas mafia and a friend of Jack Ruby.

The House Select Committee on Assassinations (HSCA), which released the report on its investigation of the JFK assassination in 1979, waded into the tangle of relationships between Jack Ruby, a weird bird/mafia associate who had ties to Santo Trafficante and Sam Giancana, to name a few; and Joseph Civello, who had been the head of the Dallas mafia since 1956, the year before he attended the infamous Apalachin Meeting; and Carlos Marcello, the head of the New Orleans mafia whose hatred of the Kennedys was well documented.

The HSCA was intrigued by the idea of some sort of mafia-involved conspiracy, but in the end, they couldn't put all the pieces together: "Oswald and Ruby showed a variety of relationships that may have matured into an assassination conspiracy," but the committee was "unable firmly to identify the other gunman or the nature and extent" of a conspiracy involving organized crime.[249]

But let us return to the FBI file, with its list of "Notorious Places of Amusement and Criminal Hangouts," which reads like the lyrics to a decadent jazz tune. Sol's Turf Bar, Club Montmarte, Apollo Club, George's Café, Best Café and the Flame were all owned by gamblers and were frequented by gamblers and other suspect individuals. Known "queer hangouts" included Le Pigalle, Gene's Music Bar, Rubaiyat, Player's Lounge and Villa Fontana. The report claimed that "no known houses of prostitution" were known to be in operation, but prostitutes were working out of a half dozen or more clubs and restaurants, including the Carousel Coffee House, the former location of Ruby's Carousel Club. Another was the Colony Club, located next door and owned by Abe Weinstein.

One of the dancers at the Colony Club was Beverly Oliver, the former mob moll who nominated Tim Overton and Jerry Ray James to the JFK conspiracy club, and by so doing, enriched the assassination gumbo with a combo of sex, Jesus, heroin, Elvis, murder, Vegas and a vast maze of Dixie Mafia connections.

Even in the alternate universe of JFK conspiracy buffs, Oliver, who now goes by the name Beverly Oliver Massegee, might strike some as a quirky, almost tragicomic figure. Others, notably JFK conspiracy author Jim Marrs and filmmaker Oliver Stone, appear to have found her stories quite credible. Beverly Oliver plays a prominent role in Stone's *JFK*. The actress Lolita Davidovitch plays her in the film.

According to Beverly Oliver's bio, she won her first talent show at the age of nine, made her nightclub debut at thirteen, moved on to the Cowtown Hoedown, Big D Jamboree and Grand Ol' Opry and from there to "traveling worldwide on the Playboy and supper club circuits." [250]

In 1963, at the age of seventeen, she was a dancer at the Colony Club. Although she was friends with Jack Ruby and other gangsters and even married one, she didn't testify before the Warren Commission, wasn't as well known as Carousel dancers like Candy Barr and Jada Conforto and didn't come forward with her story until 1970.

Oliver volunteered two roles for herself in the assassination drama. First, she claimed that she was in Dealey Plaza on November 22, 1963, wearing a tri-fold scarf on her head, filming the presidential motorcade with a Super-8 Yashica home movie camera. The identity of the woman with the scarf—the mysterious "Babushka Lady" (for the style of scarf)—had previously been unknown to assassination researchers. Oliver claimed that an FBI agent had confiscated the camera and never returned it.

For Oliver's second role, she described a dinner conversation with Tim Overton, Jerry Ray James and several organized crime figures in Dallas, whose reaction to hearing of her experience in Dealey Plaza on November 22, 1963, made her feel threatened.

One of those other crime figures was Oliver's husband, George Albert McGann. They had married in 1966. McGann was a gambler from Big Spring, Texas, a heister and Dixie Mafia contract killer. McGann was killed during a poker game in Lubbock on September 30, 1970.

Heroin wasn't working out for Oliver, so she sought solace in religion. A preacher introduced her to JFK conspiracy author J. Gary Shaw, who co-authored a book with Larry L. Harris titled *Cover-Up: The Government Conspiracy to Conceal the Facts About the Public Execution of John Kennedy*, published in 1976. Shaw subsequently interviewed Oliver and announced that the "Babushka Lady" had at last been found.

In a videotaped interview in 1993, Beverly provided the following story, mentioning Timmy Overton and Jerry Ray James, among others.[251]

> *My first husband* [George Albert McGann] *was one of the alleged leaders of the Dixie Mafia, he was a hit man…One night after a cozy little meeting at the Egyptian Lounge, an Italian restaurant here in Dallas, with a bunch of people such as Charles Harrelson, Russell Douglas Matthews, Joe and Sam Campisi, Timmy Overton, and Jerry Ray James I know for sure were there at that meeting. And I don't know how, so I can't put it all together for you, but the subject came up that I was there when it happened, you know, and I started to tell them what I saw.*
>
> *Yeah, they were friends of my husband. As a matter of fact, R.D. Matthews…was the best man at our wedding. Everybody gets this hushed attitude and they get angry and my husband just politely takes me by the arm, we are leaving and we go home and at which time he tells me I am not to mention the subject of the assassination of President Kennedy again, and at the same time I had those little buttons, campaign buttons and I had a bumper sticker, and just a bunch of little pictures and stuff and hand out bills, and he burnt them, every one of them in the fireplace.*

At this point, the videographer asked Oliver if her life had been threatened. "They just told me I wouldn't see the sunrise again," she said. Asked if she took the threat seriously, she answered, "Well, at that time he had been filed on, let's see, for the murder of Johnny Janiro; he had been filed on for the murder of Jack Kelly. I had reason to believe he was serious."

Were they serious or were they joking? According to the FBI, George McGann—a gambler, a con man and a contract killer—always carried a Thompson submachine gun in his trunk. Sheriff Buford Pusser of *Walking Tall* fame claimed that McGann was one of the four gunmen who ambushed his patrol car on New Hope Road in 1967. Pusser survived the attack, but his wife, Pauline, was killed.

Charles V. Harrelson is probably best known as the father of actor Woody Harrelson and was convicted of killing federal judge John H. Wood Jr. for a fee of $250,000, paid by El Paso drug smuggling kingpin Jimmy Chagra. When he was arrested for the murder (not his first murder-for-hire charge, either), Harrelson admitted to killing the judge and also confessed that he had killed JFK. Harrelson later denied that he had committed either killing, saying that he was out of his mind on cocaine at the time, which was, in its own way, a great piece of black comedy. Fringe conspiracy buffs have also suggested that Harrelson might have been one of the mysterious "Three Tramps" suspected of being CIA operatives in Dallas on November 22, 1963.

R.D. Matthews was a decorated veteran of World War II, also a major figure in the Dallas underworld going back to Bennie Binion's reign as kingpin of the rackets there. Matthews was the best man at Beverly and George's wedding.

Joe and Sam Campisi, as mentioned previously, owned the Egyptian Lounge, a noted character hangout. Jack Ruby was tight with the Campisis. Ruby ate a steak there the night before Kennedy was assassinated, and within a week after Ruby shot Oswald, Joe came to visit him in jail.[252] After the death of Joseph Ianni in 1973, Joe Campisi took over as head of the Dallas mafia.

This brings us to Oliver's other big claim: that Tim Overton, Jerry Ray James and other underworld characters threatened her life after hearing her JFK story. But according to a series of FBI reports from 1967 to '68, on the night in question at the Egyptian Lounge, Oliver herself might have been the most lethal person in the room. Even McGann was scared of her.

The reports were part of an interstate theft investigation: several trucks carrying a total of 126 Magnavox TV sets had been hijacked. George McGann, R.D. Matthews and a lot of other hoods in Dallas were selling them or giving them to their stripper girlfriends, admonishing the recipients "if it breaks, don't take it to no repair shop."

One of the government witnesses in the case was McGann's girlfriend, a dancer named Carolyn Gallagher. Gallagher danced at a place called the Jet Strip, where they knew her as Kari Kastle. In mid-1968, Special Agent William B. Holloman wrote to Director J. Edgar Hoover that Gallagher seemed to be losing her nerve about testifying. Chief among her concerns, it seems, were things McGann said about his wife, namely that "Beverly is crazy and that if Gallagher testifies against McGann, Beverly will kill her."

McGann also told Gallagher that at one point "he had to commit his wife Beverly to Parkland Hospital, and that she was crazy." Again, Agent Holloman repeated McGann's claim that Oliver would kill Gallagher if she testified.

Unless McGann was brazenly exaggerating his wife's eccentricities to scare his mistress into silence, his concerns about Oliver's mental stability appear to have been well founded. Recently, Gallagher said, Oliver had taken McGann's Tommy gun and was "running up and down the street where they live, shooting into houses."[253]

The year 1970, in which McGann was murdered, was a bizarre but pivotal time for Oliver. The chronology in her memoir is a little hard to follow, but she says that she was mainlining heroin four times a day, and with the help of prayer, she quit by going cold turkey. By the end of the year, she'd made a religious conversion and married a traveling evangelist named Charles Massegee. According to Massegee's website, he specializes in "Harvest Revivals, Spiritual Renewals, End Time Revivals, Crusades, and Revelation Bible Conferences."

A recent glance at Oliver's Facebook page showed that in 2014, she is still in the entertainment business, traveling the circuit from the Bible Belt to Vegas, taking bows as the JFL Conspiracy Queen/Babushka Lady and the ex-mob moll, singing and dancing, praising God and performing with the most obese Elvis tribute artists I've ever seen.

# Other Sources on the Dixie Mafia

*Mississippi Mud: Southern Justice and the Dixie Mafia*, by Edward Humes, is an excellent account of murder, gambling and corruption involving the Dixie Mafia in Biloxi, Mississippi, in the 1980s. Although there's not a lot of crossover with the Overton/James gang of the '60s, it's a great primer on the Dixie Mafia of later years.

One of the biggest Dixie Mafia stories of all was the assassination of federal district judge John H. Wood on May 29, 1979. Wood had acquired the nickname "Maximum John" because of his record of handing down harsh sentences to drug offenders. The FBI referred to the killing as "the crime of the century," launching the largest investigation since the Kennedy assassination, at a cost of over $5 million.

Tim Overton was dead by 1979, but several members of his circle—including Fat Jerry, Travis Erwin and others—had roles in the assassination of Judge John H. Wood, in the federal investigation or the trials. The best book about the case is *Dirty Dealing: Drug Smuggling on the Mexican Border and the Assassination of a Federal Judge*, by Gary Cartwright.[254]

Probably the best film about the Dixie Mafia is *Walking Tall* (1973), which was loosely based on the saga of Sheriff Buford Pusser of McNairy County, Tennessee, and his one-man war against the State Line Mob. Several of Pusser's antagonists had working relationships with Tim Overton and others mentioned here.

# Notes

## Introduction

1. *The Cactus: University of Texas 1960* (Austin: Texas Student Publications, Incorporated, 1960), 168; Robert C. Gallagher, *Ernie Davis: The Elmira Express* (Washington, D.C.: Bartleby Press, 1983), 74–75; Gary Youmans and Maury Youmans, *'59: The Story of the 1959 Syracuse University National Championship Football Team* (Syracuse, NY: Campbell Road Press, 2003), 200–05.
2. Gerry Storm, "Austin Music '65–69," http://www.texasghetto.org/Music6569.htm (accessed November 3, 2014).
3. Nick Kralj, interview with the author, 2010.
4. Nat Henderson, "Police Feel Deaths Gang Action," *Austin (TX) American-Statesman*, August 13, 1976, 1; Nat Henderson, "Austin Underworld of the '60s: Overton Gang Capers Recalled," *Austin (TX) American-Statesman*, August 13, 1976, 1.
5. *Schnautz v. United States*, 263 F.2d 525 (1959).
6. Glen Garvin and Linda Anthony, "Nelson Money Involved in Massage Parlor Deal," *Austin (TX) American-Statesman*, February 25, 1977, 1.
7. Roy Q. Minton, interview with the author, 2010.
8. Betty King, interview with the author, 2010.
9. Ibid.
10. Bernie Ward, *Dixie Mafia Intelligence Report* (Topeka, KS: Office of the Attorney General, 1974), 7–8.

# Chapter 1

11. "East First Street," Austin Public Library, http://www.austinlibrary.com/ahc/streets/1st.htm (accessed September 1, 2014).

12. Charlotte Moore, "Austin's Defining Moments," *Austin Monthly.com*, February 2014, http://www.austinmonthly.com/AM/February-2014/Defining-Moments (accessed November 3, 2014).

13. Dick DeGuerin, interview with the author, 2003.

14. Mildred Green, interview with the author, 2011.

15. Ed Wendler, interview with the author, 2004.

16. "Overton, Finus E.," *Austin City Directory* (Dallas, TX: Mitchell and Fourmby, 1940–1953).

17. TheLivingNewDeal.com, http://livingnewdeal.org/projects/chalmers-court-austin-tx (accessed November 3, 2014).

18. The original flat roofs have since been replaced with peaked roofs, which would make rooftop sleeping considerably more hazardous.

19. Green, interview, 2011.

20. Death Certificate for Ima Nell Overton, September 12, 1957, file no. 51925, Texas Department of Health, Bureau of Vital Statistics.

21. Manuel Estrada, interview with the author, 2004.

22. Bob Halford, "Maroons Poised for Title Bid," *Austin (TX) Statesman*, September 6, 1957.

23. Kay Beasley, interview with the author, 2009.

24. "Ima Nell Overton," Obituary, *(Austin, TX) American-Statesman*, September 9, 1957.

25. Walter Dollar, interview with the author, 2004.

26. Eddie Hughes, "Loss Hard for Austin; 'They Just Wanted It,'" *(Austin, TX) American-Statesman*, December 15, 1957.

27. Estrada, interview, 2004.

28. Eddie Wilson, interview with the author, 2003–04.

29. Ronnie Smith, interview with the author, 2003.

30. "Oklahoma Sooners Media Guide," https://web.archive.org/web/20070718203803/http://graphics.fansonly.com/schools/okla-dump/pdf_files/40833.pdf (accessed August 13, 2014); Sports Reference–College Football, http://www.sports-reference.com/cfb/schools/texas/1956.html (accessed August 13, 2014).

31. Beasley, interview, 2009.

32. Jimmy Banks, *The Darrell Royal Story* (Austin, TX: Eaken Press, 1973).

33. *Brownwood Bulletin*, "Austin High Grid Stars Pick Tex. U," April 16, 1958.

34. "Testimony of Florine Craine," in *James*, 432 F.2d at 2695–2700.

35. Green, interview, 2011.

36. *Waco (TX) News Tribune*, "Four Tigers Make All-District," December 9, 1957.

37. G.W. Martin, interview with the author, 2004.

38. *Cactus: The University of Texas*, 168.

39. Charles Schotz, interview with the author, 2004.

40. "Ex-Gridster Charged in Burglary," *Austin (TX) American-Statesman*, March 2, 1963.

41. Ibid.

42. Broken Spoke, http://www.brokenspokeaustintx.com (accessed September 2, 2014).

43. Bill Woods, "2ⁿᵈ Chance Not Enough for Ex-Boxer," *Austin (TX) American-Statesman*, December 15, 1960.

44. Martin, interview, 2004.

45. Pete Johnson, interview with the author, 2009.

46. Jackson, interview, 2003–04.

47. Gary M. Lavergne, *A Sniper in the Tower* (Denton: University of North Texas Press, 1997).

48. Ibid., 19–23.

49. Kralj, interview, 2010.

50. Lavergne, *Sniper in the Tower*, 19–23. Lavergne quotes one of Whitman's friends, saying that he went to the district attorney's office and swore out a peace bond against the Overtons, but the fact is, peace bonds are issued by the justice of the peace in the appropriate precinct, not by the district attorney. A search of precinct offices where a peace bond would have been properly filed turned up nothing.

51. Ibid., 22–23.

52. "Presentence Report for James Timothy Overton," in *James*, 432 F.2d 303.

# Chapter 2

53. "Ex-Gridster Charged," March 2, 1963.

54. Joye Nall, interview with the author, 2005.

55. "Presentence Report for Jerry Ray James," in *James*, 432 F.2d 303.

56. *Abilene (TX) Reporter-News*, "Burglary Charges, 5 of 7 Freed on Bonds," February 8, 1958.

57. *Abilene Reporter-News*, "Probation Revoked in Burglary Case," August 7, 1959.

58. King, interview, 2010.

59. Federal Bureau of Investigation, case no. 91-3103, FOIA request, FBI Airtel memorandum, addressed from "SAC, Dallas 91-3103 [the FBI Special Agent in charge of the Jerry Ray James fugitive case in the Dallas office]," to "Director, FBI (91-24022) (Washington, D.C., July 3, 1967).

60. *Abilene Reporter-News*, "Cooper, Hedges Pace Bulldogs on Offense," November 15, 1956.

61. *Odessa (TX) American*, "Saturday's GG Results," February 8, 1959; *Odessa American*, "Final Results," February 9, 1960.

62. *Odessa American*, "More May Be Arrested—8 Persons Involved in Burglary Series," February 9, 1961; *Odessa American*, "Burglary Suspects—Three Teen-Age Girls Released," February 10, 1961.

63. "Fred Clinton Hedges College Transcripts," in *James*, 432 F.2d 303.

64. *Tucson (AZ) Daily Citizen*, "Police Seize 12 in Texas Gambling, Dope Raid," January 14, 1963.

65. *Odessa American*, "Austin Man Held in Jail," March 19, 1963.

66. King, interview, 2010.

67. Carol A. Lipscomb, "Karankawa Indians," Handbook of Texas Online, Texas State Historical Association (http://www.tshaonline.org/handbook/online/articles/bmk05), accessed November 19, 2014. Uploaded on June 15, 2010. Published by the Texas State Historical Association.

68. Jay Harrison, interview with the author, 2004.

69. R.E. "Ernie" Scholl, interview with the author, 2004; *Austin (TX) American-Statesman*, "Burglars Escape with $50,000 Haul," August 29, 1962, 1.

70. Florine Craine, Government Tender Number [illegible], dated April 9, 1968, in *James*, 432 F.2d 303.

71. Ibid.

72. Anonymous daughters of Sue Overton, interview with the author, 2010.

73. *Seguin Gazette*, "Courthouse News: Marriage Licenses Issued at the County Clerk's Office: James Timothy Overton and Mrs. Sue Jean Smith," October 9, 1963; *Austin (TX) Statesman*, "Prostitute Role Told by Witness," April 10, 1968; Testimony of Florine Craine, *U.S. v. James (1970)*, 2665–2702.

74. Thorne Dreyer, interview with the author, 2014.

75. *Galveston Daily News Texan*, "Singer Had Gun, Arrested," September 15, 1960.

76. "Robert Ernie Scholl," Obituary, January 30, 2014, http://herald-zeitung.com/obituaries/article_5906f0dc-897d-11e3-9dec-0019bb2963f4.html (accessed November 4, 2014).

77. Scholl, interview, 2004.

78. *Austin (TX) Statesman*, "Dope Raid Nets Elite of City's Underworld," September 27, 1963, 1.

79. *Austin (TX) Statesman*, "Seven Jailed in Dope Raid at Mansfield Dam," October 2, 1963.

80. "Kennedy Assassination," *Handbook of Texas Online*, http://www.tshaonline.org/handbook/online/articles/jdk01 (accessed November 04, 2014). Uploaded on June 15, 2010. Published by the Texas State Historical Association.

81. Robert M. Barrett, "Crime Conditions in the Dallas Division," memo for the Federal Bureau of Investigation, NARA record no. 124–90091–10022, September 15, 1964. John F. Kennedy Assassination Records Collection, Mary Ferrell Foundation, 14.

# CHAPTER 3

82. Ed Magnuson and Mark Sullivan, "Texas: Where Myth and Reality Merge," *Time*, January 17, 1964, 19.

83. Ibid.

84. Jackson, interview, 2004.

85. Emmett Shelton, "Hattie Valdes," Oral history, Austin History Center, 1983.

86. *Laredo (TX) Times*, "Curry Gets Six Months in Dope Case," December 15, 1961, 6; *Laredo Times*, "New Trials Bring Shorter Sentences," 4.

87. Robert A. Burns, "Musclebound Madness at the Coliseum," *Free & Easy*, September 15, 1974; Pete Szilagyi, "A Man with Macho," *Free & Easy*, April 15, 1976.

88. Janice Farmer, interview with the author, 2011.

89. *Abilene Reporter-News*, "3 Accused in $6,000 Crime," January 30, 1964.
90. WestTexasScoutingHistory.net, http://www.westtexasscoutinghistory.net/award_eagle_cvc.html (accessed November 4, 2014); "Land Office Quiz Resumed," *Corpus Christi (TX) Caller Times*, May 18, 1955; James R. Crenshaw, "John Webster Flanagan," Drug Enforcement Administration, Department of Justice, July 15, 1975.
91. Jackson, interview, 2003–04.
92. Dorothy Brown, interview with the author, 2004.
93. Scholl, interview, 2004; "2nd Suspect in Rape Held," *Austin (TX) Statesman*, October 3, 1963.
94. Margaret Moser, "Bright Lights, Inner City," *Austin (TX) Chronicle*, July 4, 2003.
95. *Indianapolis Recorder*, "Minor Operation Fatal to Fried Chicken King," July 26, 1941.
96. Of all the music history written about Austin, the thematic connection between the Austin and Chicago places named "Ernie's Chicken Shack" seems to have been lost. I have never seen this fact mentioned before. Perhaps it was noted decades ago and then forgotten.
97. *Austin (TX) Statesman*, "Hattie Valdes Beaten, Robbed of $4,000 Cash, $5,500 Jewelry," April 3, 1964.
98. Loretta Overton, "Trial in El Paso: Woman Says She Saw Men with Guns and Bank Loot," *El Paso (TX) Herald-Post*, April 10, 1968, 1.
99. Ann Miller Strom, "Kyle, TX," *Handbook of Texas Online*, Texas State Historical Association, http://www.tshaonline.org/handbook/online/articles/hjk08 (accessed August 29, 2014).
100. Vivian Elizabeth Smyrl, "Oglesby, TX," *Handbook of Texas Online*, Texas State Historical Association, http://www.tshaonline.org/handbook/online/articles/hlo08 (accessed August 29, 2014). Uploaded on June 15, 2010. Published by the Texas State Historical Association.
101. *Austin (TX) Statesman*, "Game Parking, Traffic Take Many Policemen," November 25, 1964.
102. *Austin (TX) Statesman*, "Co-Op Safe Haul Said The Biggest," December 2, 1964.

# CHAPTER 4

103. Burglars had previously hit the bank on March 5, 1964. On that occasion, an acetylene torch was used on the vault, and the resulting fire caused extensive damage. A new vault and safe were installed afterward. In the second burglary, the new vault was broken into but not the safe. *Mexia (TX) Daily News*, "Burglars Enter Bank at Kosse During Night," February 12, 1964; *Mexia Daily News*, "Burglars Enter Kosse Bank for Second Time," March 5, 1965.
104. Scholl, interview, 2004; "Government's Reply to Motions for Acquittal," in *James*, 432 F.2d 303.
105. "Testimony of Richard Hinton," in *James*, 432 F.2d at 3809–14.
106. "Indictment," in *James*, 432 F.2d 303.

107. "Cannonball Safe," Keypicking.com, http://www.keypicking.com/viewtopic.php?f=100&t=3830 (accessed November 5, 2014).
108. *Clovis (NM) News Journal*, "Unopened Safe Dumped Claims Man," April 24, 1968; Testimony of Florine Craine, *U.S. v. James (1970)*, 2625–30; Testimony of James W. Lloyd, *U.S. v. James (1970)*, 3197–3275.
109. Jackson, interview, 2003–04; Scholl, interview, 2004; Gann, interview, 2004.
110. FBI notes of interview with Joan Taylor, in *James*, 432 F.2d.
111. "Notes from Interview with Lt. Roland W. Yarberry, Gov't Tender No. 40," in *James*, 432 F.2d 303; *El Paso Herald-Post*, "Gang Kept Under Surveillance," April 24, 1968, 6.
112. "FBI report, SA Frederick A. Jones and SA Wayne W. Wesley, May 14, 1968," in *James*, 432 F.2d 303.
113. "Testimony of Bernice James," in *James*, 432 F.2d at 5845.
114. Scholl, interview, 2004.

# CHAPTER 5

115. "History of Marihuana Legislation," http://www.druglibrary.org/schaffer/library/studies/nc/nc2_7.htm (accessed September 12, 2014).
116. Federal Bureau of Investigation report, from the field office in Dallas, TX, to San Antonio, TX, and Fort Worth, TX, Re: [redacted]; Clifford Henry Bowen; [redacted]; James Timothy Overton; William Robert Brown; the First State Bank, Mobeetie, Texas, 3/16/66, BB" April 8, 19666, 220.
117. Scholl, interview, 2004; Nat Henderson, "U.S. Court Suit Charges: His Home Bugged; Tim Overton Claims Civil Rights Violated," *Austin (TX) Statesman*, July 16, 1965; Nat Henderson, "Rights Case Deposition by Hullum Saturday," *Austin (TX) Statesman*, September 30, 1965.
118. Scholl, interview, 2004.
119. "Criminal Offense Report No. 108221, State of Texas M.O. Section, Identification and Criminal Records Division, Austin, June 8, 1965," in *James*, 432 F.2d 303.
120. Scholl, interview, 2004; Henderson, "US Court Suit."
121. Farmer, interview, 2011.
122. Storm, "Austin Music '65–69."
123. Henderson, "US Court Suit."
124. Ibid.
125. Jim Berry, "Gangsterism—Austin Style: One Night at Hattie's," *Austin (TX) Statesman*, July 16, 1965, 1.
126. Robert A. Burns, "Disorganized Crime: The Legendary Capers of Tim Overton's Gang," *Free & Easy*, January 15–February 15, 1975; Robert A. Burns, "Hattie & Peggy: You Just Can't Keep a Good Woman Down," *Free & Easy*, May 15–June 15, 1975.
127. Nat Henderson, "Madam to Testify in Ex-Mayor Hoover's Trial: Hattie Back in the Limelight," *Austin (TX) Statesman*, October 14, 1964, 1.

128. *Austin (TX) American*, "Lang Closes 'Call Houses,' Says They Will Stay Closed," January 15, 1953.

129. *(Austin, TX) Statesman*, "Hattie Valdes Declares Herself Out of Business," October 28, 1955.

130. *Denton (TX) Record-Chronicle*, "Austin Landmark Goes Up in Flames," March 16, 1961.

131. *Odessa American*, "Houston Man Faces Charges," January 5, 1960.

132. Ed Magnuson and Mark Sullivan, "Texas: Where Myth and Reality Merge," *Time*, January 17, 1964, 19.

133. Scholl, interview, 2004.

134. This number did not take into account all the other vehicles that were registered under other identities and covers. Shortly after the story was published, Overton remarked to his old friend Charles Schotz that he was driving "one of my six Cadillacs" and laughed, knowing that the others present knew he was referring to the *Statesman* story.

135. Glen Castlebury, "Sheriff Relates Deal Try," *Austin (TX) Statesman*, July 17, 1965.

136. Crenshaw, "John Webster Flanagan."

137. Carol McMurtry, "Attorney Blames Sheriff, Courthouse 'Bugged,' 'Any Home, Car, Office, Phone, Can Be Targeted,'" *Austin (TX) Statesman*, July 19, 1965; "Commissioners See Equipment, Jailhouse Visit," *Austin (TX) Statesman*, July 19, 1965; Nat Henderson, "FBI Probe of Bugging Ordered," *Austin (TX) Statesman*, July 19, 1965.

138. Henderson, "FBI Probe."

139. *Austin (TX) Statesman*, "Gun-Toting Overton Holds Police at Bay Twice," September 30, 1965.

140. Federal Bureau of Investigation report, from the field office in Dallas, TX, to San Antonio, TX, and Fort Worth, TX, "Report of [redacted], Field Office File No. 91-3103; Bureau File No. 91-24022RE: [redacted]; aka [redacted]; Clifford Henry Bowen, aka Cowan Wright; [redacted]; Unsubs (2); the First State Bank of Mobeetie, Mobeetie, Texas, 3/16/66; Bank Burglary," July 20, 1967, 5–6.

141. George Carter, "Austin Base for Thugs: Gangs Reported Working Varied Crimes in State," *Dallas (TX) Times Herald*, November 16, 1965.

142. Jim Berry, "Chief Wonders About Report: What Crime Center Here?" *Austin (TX) Statesman*, November 17, 1965.

143. Lloyd Matthews, "Miles Shuns Crime Report: 'Enough Thugs in Dallas without Help from Austin," *Austin (TX) American*, January 12, 1966.

144. Glen Castlebury, "Are Thugs Based Here? Mayor Seeks Report on Crime in Austin," *Austin (TX) Statesman*, January 17, 1966.

145. *Austin (TX) Statesman*, "Criminals Said Organizing Here," November 18, 1965; *Dallas Times Herald*, "Crime Fight Being Mapped in Austin," November 18, 1965; *Austin (TX) Statesman*, "Bechtol to Head New Grand Jury Association," December 8, 1965; *Austin (TX) Statesman*, "Court Cost Goal: Two Civic Groups Seek Gann Funds," March 6, 1966.

146. *Austin (TX) Statesman*, "Mayor Defends New Ordinance," May 21, 1968; Chris Whitcraft, "Anti-Housing Try Called Desperate by Minister," *Austin (TX) Statesman*, May 25, 1968; Minton, interview, 2010; Hub "Big Boy" Bechtol, National Football Foundation, http://www.footballfoundation.org/Programs/CollegeFootballHallofFame/SearchDetail.aspx?id=40059 (accessed November 6, 2014).

## CHAPTER 6

147. Wendler, interview, 2004.

148. Scholl, interview, 2004; Jackson, interview, 2003–04.

149. *Austin (TX) Statesman*, "Bullet in Back: Ex-Con Shot, Suspect Held," January 13, 1966.

150. *Austin (TX) American*, "Overton and Lawyer Nabbed in Burglaries," January 20, 1966, 1.

151. *United States v. James Timothy Overton*, United States District Court, Western Division, San Antonio, TX, no. 67-129-SA (1968).

152. Morton P. Chiles, FD-302 report, Federal Bureau of Investigation, February 23, 1966.

153. Jerry Wix Lemond, Findagrave.com (accessed November 6, 2014).

154. "Agent R.E. Scholl to Agent in Charge W.E. Naylor, Texas Department of Public Safety, Interoffice Memorandum, Aug. 31, 1965," in *James*, 432 F.2d 303; Scholl, interview, 2004.

155. Jerry Ray James was driving the same model car in December 1963 or early 1964, according to statements by Florine Craine. She remembered seeing James for the first time (shortly after the Kennedy assassination, she said), at the Transmission Exchange, where Snooks did some repairs on it. "FBI interview with Florine Craine, April 9, 1968," in *James*, 432 F.2d 303.

156. Court of Criminal Appeals of Texas, reply to "Ex Parte, Jimmy Taylor, Darrell Wayne Overton and Mildred Ross, No. 39,560, 147th Judicial District, Travis County, Texas," March 23, 1966.

157. Federal Bureau of Investigation report, from Special Agent in charge, San Antonio to Director, FBI, "Report of [redacted], Field Office File No. 91-24022RE: [redacted]; aka [redacted]; Clifford Henry Bowen, aka Cowan Wright; [redacted]; Unsubs (2); the First State Bank of Mobeetie, Mobeetie, Texas, 3/16/66, BB," March 17. 1966.

158. Ibid.

159. *Corsicana (TX) Daily News*, "Bloodhounds Searching for Bank Burglars," March 17, 1966, 1; *Austin (TX) Statesman*, "3 Held, 2 Hunted in Bank Burglary," March 17, 1966, 8; *Wheeler (TX) Times*, "Bank Robbery Attempt Fails," March 17, 1966, 1; *Austin (TX) Statesman*, "Austin Man Captured as Bank Burglary Suspect, Four of Five Now in Custody," March 18, 1966; *Austin (TX) Statesman*, "Tim Overton Held in Bank Burglary," March 19, 1966.

160. "Affidavit for Search Warrant Signed by Amarillo Detective Arthur Fields, March 19, 1966," *James*, 432 F.2d 303.

161. Tony Proffitt and Lloyd Mathews, "Two Bodies Found in Austin Finally Identified as Missing Sorority Girls," *Austin (TX) Statesman*, July 31, 1965, 1.

162. James Langdon, "Langdon's Nightbeat," *Austin (TX) Statesman*, December 11, 1965.

163. James Langdon, "Ban on Record Here Somewhat Strange," *Austin (TX) Statesman*, January 27, 1966; *Austin (TX) Statesman*, "Five Charged Here in Dope Possession," January 28, 1966.

164. Thorne Dreyer, "The Spies of Texas," *Texas Observer*, November 17, 2006.

## CHAPTER 7

165. Cheryl Smith, "Everything Old Is New Again: 'The Rag' Returns to Austin," *Austin Chronicle*, September 2, 2005.

166. Wilson, interview, 2003–04.

167. Minton, interview, 2010.

168. Edward Humes, *Mississippi Mud* (New York: Pocket Books, 1995), 395–96.

169. "Testimony of Bernice James," in *James*, 432 F.2d at 5845–5911.

170. "Testimony of Betty Joyce Dabbs," in *James*, 432 F.2d at 6032–58, 6476–6500, 6068–6200.

171. *Brownsville (TX) Herald*, "Corpus Christi Slick Makes it to Top Ten," August 17, 1966.

172. Ward, "Dixie Mafia," 1–25, 74–76.

173. Ibid., 26–32.

174. Gann, interview, 2004.

175. Scholl, interview, 2004.

176. *Austin (TX) Statesman*, "Tim Overton Charged Anew," May 16, 1967.

177. King, interview, 2010.

178. *Amarillo (TX) Globe-Times*, "Three Say 'Guilty' in Bank Job," April 24, 1967.

179. As vice president, LBJ lobbied successfully for the appointment of Hughes, and JFK appointed her in 1961. She was the first female federal judge. Among her notable rulings was *Roe v. Wade*, legalizing abortion for women in the United States. Robert S. La Forte, "Hughes, Sarah Tilghman," *Handbook of Texas Online*, http://www.tshaonline.org/handbook/online/articles/fhu68 (accessed November 08, 2014). Uploaded on June 15, 2010. Published by the Texas State Historical Association.

180. Gary Cartwright, *Dirty Dealing: Drug Smuggling on the Mexican Border and the Assassination of a Federal Judge* (New York: Atheneum, 1984), 229.

## CHAPTER 8

181. *Odessa American*, "Defense Attorney Estimates Conspiracy Case Cost $1.5 Million," June 26, 1968.

182. "Indictment," in *James*, 432 F.2d 303.

183. "Gov't Reply to Motions, June 14, 1968," in *James*, 432 F.2d 303; "Subpoena Addressed R.E. Scholl," in *James*, 432 F.2d at 303.

184. "Govt's Closing Argument," in *James*, 432 F.2d at 8500–24.

185. *James*, 432 F.2d at 2646–50; Berry, "Gangsterism"; King, interview, 2010.

186. "Testimony of Florine Craine," in *James*, 432 F.2d at 2611–2640, 2800.

187. *Odessa American*, "Gang Members Menace Media in Del Rio Court," February 20, 1968, 20; *Amarillo Globe-Times*, "Newsmen Cursed at Criminal Hearing," February 20, 1968; *Del Rio (TX) News-Herald*, "Prisoners Spit, Kick Reporters," February 19, 1968.

188. "Motion for the Release of Items in the Custody of the Clerk at Del Rio," in *James*, 432 F.2d 303.

189. Heygood Gulley, interview with the author, 2010.

190. George Thurmond, interview with the author, 2010.

191. *James*, 432 F.2d at 6308–15.

192. "Testimony of John W. Flanagan," in *James*, 432 F.2d at 663–82.

193. Nat Henderson, "Five Officers Deny Beating of Ex-Con," *Austin (TX) Statesman*, September 29, 1965.

194. "Testimony of Robert S. Travis, George Gilkerson, Fred A. Semaan, Pat Mulloy," in *James*, 432 F.2d at 6252–6320; Vern Knickerbocker, interview with the author, 2004.

195. *Brownsville Herald*, "Play Girl Testifies On Conspiracy," May 26, 1968.

196. "Testimony of Betty Joyce Dabbs," in *James*, 432 F.2d at 6662.

197. "Gov't Reply to Motions for Acquittal, Bill of Particulars Reply to Motion by Defense to Compel Government to Reveal the Names of Unindicted Co-conspirators, List of Witnesses," in *James*, 432 F.2d 303.

198. "Secret Service Agent Indicted," *Nevada State Journal*, May 22, 1964; *United States v. Anthony D'antonio, et al*, 362 F.2d 151 (7th Cir. June 9, 1966).

199. *Austin (TX) Statesman*, "Prostitute Testifies in Conspiracy Trial," May 25, 1968; *Brownsville Herald*, "Play Girl Testifies."

200. Notes from interview with Florine Craine, Gov't Tender, April 9, 1968, in *U.S. v. James* (1970).

201. "Order Granting Motion for Mistrial and for Commitment of Defendant Mildred Ross to Medical Center for Study as to Mental Condition," in *James*, 432 F.2d 303.

202. Scholl, interview, 2004; *El Paso Herald-Post*, "Police Thwart City Jail Riot," June 3, 1968.

203. *James*, 432 F.2d at 4500–45; "Defendant Ill; Trial Recessed," *Austin (TX) Statesman*, May 5, 1968.

204. King, interview, 2010.

205. "Defense Attorney Estimates."

206. *Estes v. Texas*, 381 U.S. 532 (1965); "Billie Sol Estes," *Time*, May 25, 1962, http://content.time.com/time/covers/0,16641,19620525,00.html (accessed November 6, 2014).

# Chapter 9

207. Pete Johnson, interview with the author, 2009.

208. "Allocution Hearing, 1971," in *James*, 432 F.2d at 303.

209. Anonymous daughters of Sue Overton, interview, 2010.

210. Ward, "Dixie Mafia," 33–40.

211. Laylee Muslovski, interview with the author, 2014.

212. Debi Dabbs, interview with the author, 2014.

213. "Error Corrected in Shooting Report," *Oklahoman (OK)*, April 19, 1969.

214. *Oklahoman*, "Woman Slain; Husband Held," November 5, 1970; *Oklahoman*, "Askins Plans Release Plea in Hearing," December 8, 1970.

215. *Oklahoman*, "Bond Denied Professional Bail Maker," December 18, 1970.

216. *Oklahoman*, "Wife Killer Asks to Marry Lawyer," September 3, 1973

217. Charles Craig, interview with the author, 2009; Bob Mann, interview with the author, 2014.

218. District Clerk of Dallas County, "Larry G. Culbreath Indictment," case no. F73-04177-P, case no. 73-04178-P, April 30, 1973.

219. *Austin (TX) Statesman*, "Local 1960's Crime Figure Shot Dead," December 10, 1972.

220. Henderson, "Austin Underworld."

221. Pete Johnson, interview with the author, 2009.

222. Wilson, interview, 2003–04.

223. Cartwright, *Dirty Dealing*, 219.

224. Ward, "Dixie Mafia," 23.

225. District Clerk of Dallas County, "Larry G. Culbreath."

226. Mark Donald, "Good Time Charlie: The Don of Dallas Criminal Lawyers Charles Tessmer Reshaped Justice Trough Decades of Hard-fought Cases and Hard Drink," *Dallas (TX) Observer*, December 23, 1999.

227. Stewart Davis, "Regents Club Purchase Stirs Legislator's Ire," *Dallas (TX) Morning News*, September 30, 1972.

228. Federal Bureau of Investigation, "Subjects: Joe Campisi, Joseph Campisi," file no. 124–90021–10067, June 29, 1973, MaryFerrellfoundation.org (accessed November 6, 2014).

229. Anonymous daughters of Sue Overton, interview with the author, 2010.

230. Jack Wild (pseudonym), interview with the author, 2009.

231. *Dallas Morning News*, "Police Seek Connection in Death, Visit to DA," March 3, 1973.

232. Death Certificate for Dale Norwood Hall, March 5, 1973, file no. 18355, Texas Department of Health, Bureau of Vital Statistics.

# Chapter 10

233. Richard West, "Reporter," *Texas Monthly*, April 1976, 12.

234. Jerry Deal, "Massive Dope Ring Back in Action," *San Antonio (TX) Express-News*, May 16, 1976.

235. *(Austin, TX) Sunday American-Statesman*, "Overton Gang Member Gives Up Life of Crime for Religion," September 19, 1976.

236. Last we heard, Jerry Ray James was in the federal witness protection program, which would add some complications to the movie deal, but presumably, any difficulties could be overcome with money, lawyers and the right talent attached to the project.

237. John L. Smith, *Of Rats and Men: Oscar Goodman's Life from Mob Mouthpiece to Mayor of Las Vegas* (Las Vegas, NV: Huntington Press 2003), 125–35; "Goodman, Oscar," Wikipedia Contributors, Wikipedia, https://en.wikipedia.org/wiki/Oscar_Goodman, accessed November 22, 2014.

238. Ibid, 219.

239. James C. McKinley Jr., "Jamiel A. Chagra, 63, Drug Kingpin, Dies," *New York Times*, July 29, 2008; Cartwright, *Dirty Dealing*, 349–67.

240. Dabbs, interview, 2010.

241. District Clerk of Dallas County, "Larry G. Culbreath."

242. Federal Court docket, Larry Gale Culbreath, A-76-CR-45, May 20, 1976.

243. "Rockport Link to Probe," *Victoria (TX) Advocate*, March 23, 1981.

244. Cartwright, *Dirty Dealing*, 220.

245. Ibid, 233, 239, 330–31.

246. District Clerk of Dallas County, "Larry G. Culbreath."

# Appendix 1

247. One portal for accessing the collection is the Assassination Archive and Records Collection, http://aarclibrary.org (accessed November 17, 2014).

248. Barrett, "Crime Conditions."

249. JFK Assassination Records, Report of the Select Committee on Assassinations of the U.S. House of Representatives, http://www.archives.gov/research/jfk/select-committee-report (accessed November 17, 2014).

250. "The Life Story of Beverly Massegee: A Miracle of God's Grace," Massegee.org, http://www.massegee.org/newsRelease2.html (accessed November 14, 2014).

251. Harry A. Yardum, *The Grassy Knoll Witnesses: Who Shot JFK?* (Bloomington, IN: Authorhouse, 2009), 51–57.

252. "HSCA Appendix to Hearings," 336, http://www.aarclibrary.org/publib/jfk/hsca/reportvols/vol9/html/HSCA_Vol9_0172b.htm.

253. "George Albert McGann; Harold Mote Pruitt, aka; et al," FBI field report of SA William B. Holloman; NARA no. 15-60061-48, October 14, 1968.

# Appendix 2

254. Cartwright, *Dirty Dealing*.

# A Note on Sources

M ost of the reference notes in this book should be self-explanatory. My research into the criminal case histories began with the felony and misdemeanor files at the Travis County Courthouse and the docket sheets at the federal courthouse in Austin. Eventually, I found my way to the National Archives and Records Administration (NARA) in Fort Worth, where I located the case file for the 1968 conspiracy trial of Jerry Ray James, James Timothy Overton and eighteen others. This case file was probably the biggest single source of information for this book. All notes pertaining to the NARA file, as well as the case itself, are identified by the styling of the appellate court ruling in that case, i.e., *United States v. James*, 432 F.2d 303 (1970).

The file consists of nine thousand pages of transcript, plus hundreds of motions, briefs, FBI interview notes, criminal records, crime scene photos, mug shots, FBI memos and other materials contained in thirty-four file boxes. The file also included material from other federal court cases in Texas, such as the separate trials in the Mobeetie case in 1967. I've attempted to identify the material referenced in this file as best I could.

Summaries of appellate court decisions also provided some important facts and, occasionally, a juicy anecdote. Newspapers were especially helpful for dates, names and corroboration of other information.

I realize that human memory is an imperfect thing; therefore, information from interviews was used as judiciously as possible.

Background information on places, names and such was informed by a variety of sources, and for most Texas background history and geography, *The Handbook of Texas* was my back-up source.

I know of no other books that concentrate on the same group of subjects during the same time period as this one. As stated in the introduction, *Dirty Dealing*, by Gary Cartwright, includes bits of information about Jerry Ray James and several others mentioned in this book but not during the time period covered here.

Bernie Ward's *Dixie Mafia Intelligence Report* (Topeka, KS: Office of the Attorney General, 1974) was helpful for insights and further corroboration on a great deal of information that was originally provided by R.E. "Ernie" Scholl in interviews, which is only logical because he was well-acquainted with many, if not all, of the investigators who contributed to that report. In fact, he may even be one of several contributors who preferred to remain anonymous.

FBI reports obtained under the Freedom of Information and Privacy Act (FOIPA) are identified to the best of my ability.

# About the Author

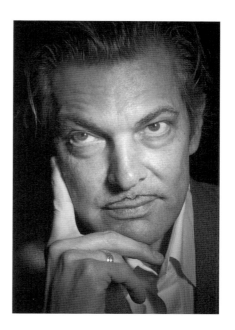

J esse Sublett is an author, musician and artist from Austin, Texas. His first published novel was *Rock Critic Murders*, released in 1989. His nonfiction books include the music and true crime memoir *Never the Same Again: A Rock n' Roll Gothic* and *Broke, Not Broken: Homer Maxey's Texas Bank War*, published by Texas Tech University Press, 2014.

He has written many history documentaries, along with feature work for *Texas Monthly*, *Texas Observer*, *New York Times*, *Texas Tribune* and *Austin Chronicle*. He is a member of the Texas Institute of Letters.

His seminal Austin rock band, the Skunks, founded in 1978, was inducted into the Austin Music Hall of Fame in 2008.

Jesse Sublett lives in Austin with his wife, Lois Richwine. His blog can be found at JesseSublett.com.